88

A Journal Of Contemporary American Poetry

Issue 3 - October 2003

Hollyridge Press
Venice, California

Managing Editor
Ian Randall Wilson

© 2003 Hollyridge Press

Hollyridge Press
P.O. Box 2872
Venice, California 90294

Cover Design by D.L. Stevens

Manufactured in the United States of America by Lightning Source

ISBN: 0-9676003-7-5

Indexed by: The American Humanities Index; The Index of American
Periodical Verse; Poem Finder on the Web; MLA Bibliography and MLA
Directory of Periodicals.

88: A Journal of Contemporary American Poetry is published annually by
Hollyridge Press. Please see the last pages of the issue for specific submission
information. Copyright reverts to authors on publication though in the event
of a reprint we ask for courtesy credit.

88's naming is something of a mystery. Some say it was named in homage
to Alfred Stieglitz's *291*. Others suggest that the numerals are taken from
the address of the editor's late relatives. Still another version is that the
upright double-infinity signs suggest boundless imagination. It just may be
that the anapest sounds good to the ear, feels good to the mouth.

Hollyridge Press is a small press publisher located in Venice, California. Using
Print-On-Demand technology, Hollyridge Press, publishes primarily literary
fiction. Print-On-Demand allows Hollyridge Press to maintain modest overhead
through low initial print costs and minimal inventory. Books are always in print
and available through wholesalers Ingram and Baker & Taylor.

Contents

Contributors
Guidelines

EDITOR'S NOTE TO THE THIRD ISSUE

What is contemporary American poetry? What is its best expression? Is its arbiter a journal such as *Poetry*, beneficiary of a hundred million dollar bequest from the granddaughter of a drug manufacturer who never had work accepted in her lifetime? I don't know the answers to these questions but I ask them because they're relevant in my understanding of how I'm putting *88* together and what role *88* has to play—if any—in the continuing dialogue about poetry. Ron Silliman, writing on his blog (ronsilliman.blogspot.com), suggested that at one time *Poetry* was publishing a kind of overview or a totality of American poetry at the moment. But it's hard to know what that means. Do you take a little lyricism from column A and a little narrative from column B and something experimental or language-centered from column C and there it is: American poetry?

From what comes in, but more directly from whom I solicit—and that solicitation is as wide as I can make it limited only by a lack of current addresses—the work featured in *88* is selected. I've been exposed to a pretty wide range of poetries and while I see my own work as a bricolage of all that exposure, I can appreciate a mainstream lyric poem as well as one the more sturdy examples of L=A=N=G=U=A=G=E poetry. What I do know is that poetry is not therapy, that the notion of "writing from heart" has always struck me as a silly one. Or perhaps it's just that I was never issued that special connecting device that allows others to shove a pen into their chest and get going. I've cringed in workshops when someone begins their critique by saying, "That was so courageous of you to read that piece." I'm with Frank O'Hara who said that he didn't care "about clarifying experiences for anyone or bettering (other than accidentally) anyone's state or social relations."

88's evolving mission is an attempt to present the broadest range of American poetry. But the filter of selection is at issue. G.W. Clift and J.E. Roper, writing in a recent issue of *Literary Magazine Review*, tell us that "it is no trick to edit a journal without standards." I agree with them completely. They go on to say that 88 is "held together by attitude and custom rather than by technique or actual social commerce." So we we'll let *attitude and custom* be our guide for now. All that outside reading—it's been worth something, apparently.

In other interesting news from the outside, three poems from the premier issue of *88* were selected by Yusef Komunyakaa for inclusion in *Best American Poetry 2003*: George Higgins' "Villanelle," Tony Hoagland's "Summer Night" and David Wagoner's "On Being Asked to Discuss Poetic Theory." Congratulations to the poets and also to Denise Stevens, managing editor of *88* for the premier issue.

In this issue, we move from ordering the poems alphabetically to a more Dada chance method, organizing the poems in the order they were accepted. Some will suggest that this process still abrogates any responsibility for considering relationships between poems, for considering how they might interact by theme or content or form. But, as a student of poststructuralism and postmodernism, I have issues about the arbitrary nature of the sign. I'd suggest that any order is arbitrary, and that notions of theme, etc. are reader-constructed, i.e., it's all in your mind. So it's Dada this time around, and whatever happy accidents ensue in the juxtaposition of poems we'll take as cosmically indicated.

—Ian Randall Wilson, Los Angeles, October 2003

Brian Clements

PLEASE HOLD DURING THE SILENCE

"The week leading up was chaos" is a way of telling what to look at, like a countdown to the first note. After two decades of reported sightings, it was starting to look like things in essence were raw blues. So we got on a plane to New York—you in your invisible shirt, everyone else wearing documentation of memorable moments.

Shortly thereafter, the music got more adventurous. Instead of leaving Fridays and coming back late Sunday, we stayed weeks at a time. The rhythm section never left. A classical penchant for the right note grew into your fingers.

Some others may think this is allegory. It's hard to speak without quoting, out of context, incessantly. There are ways to try, but those formulae prove self-defeating and they scare us.

Music and money have their own heavens, but we are a lesser species. The things that I used to do… But I got tired of being about myself, and so did she after all those guerilla landings, bopping off shot glasses like notes.

Now you can see the whole a bit better, no? This conversation began with stomping in a roadhouse. Before that, it was a pick in a minstrel's pocket. Before that, a traveling salesman wrote and named a little sonnet and sang it in public for a servant. I myself must now travel. Wait for the tone.

Peter Levitt

A STRING OF BIRDS

deft, strong,
aren't you
too old
to act
this way?

*

the poem
is not
the man
tell someone

*

hard to
wrap a sweater
around empty
arms

but girls
try every
day and die
trying

*

I lost
your poems
in the bathroom
forgive me

they were
so delicious
and so
cold

*

what now?

Peter Levitt

WOMAN WEARING PEARLS LOOKS FROM JUST-ARRIVING GUESTS AT DOORWAY, CASTS OVER-THE-SHOULDER GLANCE TOWARD HUSBAND READING IN HIS CHAIR AND SAYS, "VICTOR! IT'S THE SPOILS!" OR, MEET THE WEISENHEIMERS

my wife and friend go to an evening
of stage hypnotism where the Man
of the Evening clearly
just off a bus with his Two
High School Dropout assistants
take the Stage. The Hypnotist
does not dazzle anyone but
one of his assistants (they
both love him) spends
the evening trying to close
his lower lip. For
the grand finale
a woman comes
up from the audience
and while under His spell
lifts one hand and arm
after another while He
plucks imaginary
marionette strings.
He plucks, she lifts.
She lifts, he plucks.
Only problem is
he plucks left and
(you got it)
she lifts right. Over

and over again
while the loving
assistant tries

to get
that lip
to shut.

"Did you have a nice time?"
that's me when my wife
gets home. She tells me,
and then she says her friend
wants to go on a diet. I
run to my file-o'poems file
and pull one out
from thirty years ago,
to wit:

"You're eyelids are getting heavy."

"Too many potatoes?"

Louis Phillips

FOUND POEM #88765490

(from the index to The Letters of Jean Rhys*)*

money, 22, 47, 50, 58, 70, 74, 77,
   78, 79, 81(2), 92-3, 115, 115-16,
   119, 129, 137, 145, 147(2), 164,
   171, 180, 181(2), 188, 189, 191,
   206, 208, 239, 245, 247, 247-8, 295

Louis Phillips

THE PARTS OF A SINGLE ADJECTIVE

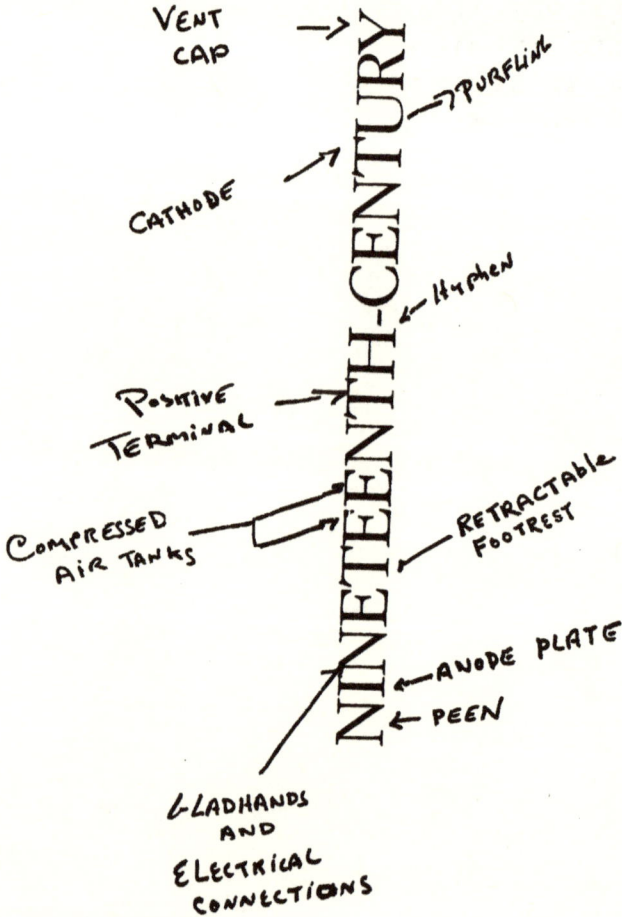

VENT CAP →

NINETEENTH-CENTURY

→ PURFLING

CATHODE ↗

← Hyphen

POSITIVE TERMINAL →

COMPRESSED AIR TANKS

← RETRACTABLE FOOTREST

← ANODE PLATE

← PEEN

L-LADHANDS AND ELECTRICAL CONNECTIONS

Louis Phillips

POETRY SELF-TAUGHT WITH PICTURES

Bright star, would I were
Steadfast as thou art

But at my back I always hear
Time's winged chariot hurrying near

Whenever Richard Corey went
down town,
We people on the pavement
looked at him

Hear the sledges with the bells,—
HATS

Silver bells!
HATS

Matt Hart

DADA'S SAWED-OFF HALF BROTHER

Take any line. Cut it off.
Take any new line, set it
to music, set it ablaze.
Watch it collapse into settle and haze
and forget about vision. Instead be prepared
to appear as applesauce. Be prepared
to tell us why you waltz. Cut it off at the
Boy Scout motto. Add the phrase,
To turn red, as in hot communista,
as in delicious suspect, as in
laundromat heaven. Cut off everything
before the word laundromat and everything
after the la of laundromat. Now sing
La Fortunato in the gutter. Now sing
Why are all the radicals crying?
Answer: Because they've lost their
shells of chocolate cool, their
yard-long tongues of provocative dust.
Make a line, if you will, a cut
in the dust. Let go of everything
but the whistle. Make it
wistful, make somebody sigh.
Make a mask out of orange mud
and scare with it. Make cry.
Use extreme caution with amputation.
Cut up and modified, one gets amplified
and putative. One begins to break. Generous
association reveals, A needle exists.
Amplify the needle, then cut it
to pieces. Am punctured, living fury.
Therefore, need lemons. My heart won't
stop crowing at the crack of dawn.
My voice won't stop cracking at the sight
of blood. O beautiful for spacious. Cut off.

Matt Hart

DIRIGIBLE. DOG BREATH. TIMBUKTU.

If you are a lava lamp, then I am a broken
heating element, then the freezer stays cooler
and we are preserved as smoldering finches
and blood oranges.

If a balloon in your mouth feels like hooray
followed by a cotton seed, followed by a tumor,
then the sanitarium is unnecessary
as you are deeply exploding.

If the report comes back, No intelligent life,
then no breath, no maraschino cherries, no
antennae, no win.

Here I can only think: clog, puff of smoke,
abstract blob of burned plastic bags.

Everything in this house of ants and lizards,
from the firecrackers down to the fat lady smoking
cigarettes on the buckling ice rink,
is conditional.

If I'm the one who never forgets, then you two
never remember.

Matt Hart

POEM

To be interested.
To seek a world of experience in superlatives
as in, Very good great radiator
as in, Wonderfully fabulous shoebox
Marvelous toadstool
Best mannequin of all…
This is the proper trajectory of living. This is the way
we make vivid mistakes.
Imagination.
Invention.
And re-invention upon re-invention.
For example, the dog again.
Or Captain Cowgill's Winter White Bean soup.
Then listening to Blossom Dearie or a hockey puck or simply
a fuck-up alone in his car.
In all things ask only for love,
in the mouth and in the mailbox.
As it happens, my tongue laps against
the hull of this rowboat.
And I wonder about these circumstances
the way I might about a theory—knowing
soon I'll move on to choicer conundrums.
How to fix my broken toaster.
And where to buy figs in the rain in Cincinnati.

Lee Rossi

REVIEW:
PITY THE BATHTUB ITS FORCED EMBRACE OF THE HUMAN FORM by MATTHEA HARVEY
Alice James Books, 2000. $14.95

In her first book, Matthea Harvey shows herself to be an enthusiastic miniaturist. Many of her poems' most persuasive moments occur outside their narrative or lyric arc in the intricate exchanges between subject and verb or word and modifier. In "The Illuminated Manuscript," for instance, one of her many personae, a master scribe, tells his apprentice, to "*look at the people / in their pews see how their slant is similar /… but a loop of hair or longer line makes all the difference*" (53). Almost by definition, poetry invites exceptional attention to each of its moments and modalities; the texture and flavors of each word are so much more important than in prose. But Harvey re-calibrates this sort of attentiveness with the electron microscope of her own sensibility to produce a fanaticism of the small.

Nowhere is this more evident than in the way she manages enjambment. A typical line will run into the next. But then the next statement will begin even while the last is still ending, almost a palimpsest. Often the effect is dizzying.

> now through
> The ice [people] saw details meadowsweets silver pussytoes &
> Thyme seemed like an appropriate thing to be trapped in
> There was a girl who loved the meadow so much that one night
> She strapped on her skates & dared to skate on it surface (15)

As readers, we struggle upstream against the downhill flow of words in order to recover our place in the swirl of meanings. The absence of punctuation and the modernist re-vision of the antique habit of capitalizing the first word of a line merely reinforce this syntactic push-pull. What emerges is not so much a Theme or even a welter of ideas, although both are part of the mix, as much as an experience of the slipperiness of language.

An abundance of ideas and thematic motifs, enough to fill a Wal-Mart, contributes as well to this impression of unmanageable riches. With a wink, perhaps, at that great master of the equivocal, Wallace Stevens, Harvey gives us a number of pieces which address the relation of visual art & writing. Her apprentice scribe says, for instance, "I thought of writing as painting's poor relation" (53). And elsewhere, in the wonderfully titled "Nude on a Horsehair Sofa by the Sea," we see the speaker "fretting over how to paint / the word *sometimes* because the pebbles / only show when the water's had a chance / to settle" (5). Perhaps it's the writer who hasn't had a chance to settle (this is, after all, a first book). In "Thermae" we see a writer in classical Rome struggle with inspiration: "Because he is thinking so hard about his ode, because his mind is full of *what if I fail, what if I can't imagine* he doesn't notice the man with the ill-fitting toga whom he would have mocked at dinner" (42). It's not just words, then, that mock our need to create (create order, Stevens would say), not just the rich and multifarious world, but our own intractable minds. Many of the poems involve a tension, almost a dialectic between creation and the uncreated, between nature and culture, art and the artist, text and interpretation, between the aestheticism she inherits from Stevens and the flippant materialism of someone like Dean Young.

There are somber notes as well. She declares, "I too am attracted to want" (58). Disappointment in love figures in a number of these poems as in "Outside the Russian / Turkish Baths" where we find two men: "The older man's confusion / becomes wonder, the younger's malice, delight, they are master / and apprentice, it is Venice, they have finally discovered how to take all the color out of glass and make it clear" (8).

For the most part, however, Harvey displays a sprightliness and vivacity that reminds one of her fellow New Yorkers Kenneth Koch and Frank O'Hara. The sound "The Oboe Player" produces "is never thin enough, / cannot express *I am a lost nymph in the woods* without adding, / *a voluptuous nymph at that*" (35).

It is hard to predict who she will become. Perhaps she will remain as protean as she currently is. Certainly exuberance is one of her strengths, as in "The Gem Is on Page Sixty-Four" where she rhapsodizes over "two boys in a basement in ecstasy over something imaginary / Which couldn't be taken away & poured down the sink" (41).

And yet mightn't we also wonder if the fickleness of the market-place hasn't infected Harvey's sense of what a poem is. There are those of us who like to suppose that poetry is somehow apart from the world of getting and spending, its omnivorous boredom. But what's a young poet to do to gain and maintain an ear-hold with an audience of poetry readers who are just as exquisitely bored as the army of Sports Center viewers (who are probably part of that army)? Certainly she could do worse than *Pity the Bathtub*, an exasperating, wonderful Scarlett O'Hara of a book that repays the extravagant expenditure of attention it demands.

Lee Rossi

REVIEW:
ROUGE PULP by DOROTHY BARRESI
University of Pittsburgh Press, 2002. $12.95

If politics is the art of the possible, then poetry is the science of the impossible, testing every theory, system, and dogma with the clenched fist of experience. In her third book, *Rouge Pulp*, Dorothy Barresi proves herself to be one of the ex-est of ex-Catholics, pulling deeply etched vignettes of suburban girlhood from an acid bath of wit and fury. These are post-feminist, post-multi-cultural poems, poems that could only have been written by someone who'd been cosseted and cozened by orthodoxies, both Right and Left. This poet's Shit Detector works overtime.

At the heart of the book is the writer's ambivalence about being a woman. There is, for instance, a series of anything-but-elegiac elegies for her mother, whose failure as a role model for a smart, rebellious daughter, leads the poet to declare, in a phrase that glee-fully up-ends Rilke, "Every good mother is terrible" (2). What she learned from her mother was how to look, how to dress, how to adorn the puzzling, impractical, female body. But what is the body for? Who is the ghost in this machine? As a wife and mother, the poet is continually asking herself what these traditional womanly roles have to do with her basic experience of disillusionment.

As the proprietor of "A Posh Salon Called Ultra" tells her, "no matter what you've heard // or believed all these years, living the life of the mind," what matters to most people is how she looks, "a plain woman despising us for what we know she lacks" (9). Chief co-conspirator with the Beauty Industry, of course, was the poet's mom, "Mother my law, my verse, my tampon,.../ my tears" (10) from whom she learned that "No woman is beautiful enough" (40). Not for her, the melancholy, yet confident assertion of Yeats's friend, "To be born a woman is to know / that we must labor to be beautiful" ("Adam's Curse").

The body is plainly at issue. But then so is most everything else in this poet's inheritance. The 50's, for one thing, with its "altar of argyle," its "windsor knot of work weeks," its "Penneys of Sears," all the familiar and stultifying icons of mass culture, but also its iconic violence, "the Enola Gay in a dandelion field,…the Edsel of Vietnam" (28). Neither does her Irishness offer this hyphenate-American any balm. "The Irish in me ride the lion of poetry / out of the desert of many pints" (15). Literature and learning also receive their portion of mockery and scorn, as in "Sock Hop with the New Critics." "The world understood," she notes, "is a *tiny* world." And more to the point, this all-male meritocracy "forgot to invite the girls" (27). Even the prior generation of women poets seems to have failed her. "The Heaven of Otto Plath," for example, is an exercise in sympathy for that villain of every a feminist's fantasy. "Who edits a parent down," she asks, "in the dark gold of her own dark stirrings?" How awful she implies to have a child (like herself?), who "wants to bloom and sting, bloom and sing, / *Look at me*" (64).

Intense and even hysterical as these poems often are, they seldom become simply apologies for the poet's eccentricities. She is too smart, too self-aware. She knows she was a screamer as a kid, and acknowledges her own prickly, withholding brand of love. In "Dorothyism," a paean to her talent for self-deception, she urges herself to "remember that you are made up of protein and bad judgment" (57). And later orders herself to "Hoe the ghost-farm daily to discourage annoying weeds— / nothing is personal. / In the end you will give back your memories / like an overdue book / and pay the fine, and walk away" (58).

What saves her, and there is a kind of redemption here, is the body, that well of frustration and unacknowledged power. In a poem addressed to her infant son, "For Dante at One," she tells him that, after a suitably difficult birth, the noise of his first cry was "more beautiful than everything I had known. / Alive together in that surgical theater, / I learned what my body is good for" (38).

Not that this knowledge makes her life is any easier; but it is different, and so is the poet. She becomes our Virgil, as we tour the various circles of our world, witnessing all the violence and pain which daily fill our consciousness. Yet despite this, she exhibits a new sense of confidence and power. In "Possibly I Have Misunderstood." she says, "When I began losing my looks / I thought, alright, good, / One less thing to worry about." Now that she's entered middle age, her youthful resentment and rebellion have toughened into a wary acceptance of her life. What she says of her women friends is equally true of her: they "hear acutely / what approaches / and are not afraid" (84).

Lee Rossi

REVIEW:
RIPE by ROY JACOBSTEIN
University of Wisconsin Press, 2002. $12.95

If Roy Jacobstein's life has been half as interesting as the Poetry Daily website suggests, it's a wonder he's written anything. A public health physician formerly with USAID, he has worked in such "far-flung" places as Tallinn, Istanbul, Kathmandu, and Phnom Penh. One thinks of William Carlos Williams making house calls in a Lear Jet. Indeed, Dr. Williams' humanity and formal restlessness seems to inform Jacobstein's first book *Ripe*, winner of the Pollak Prize.

But more than Williams, Jacobstein reminds me of Philip Levine, another poet from Detroit. In the depth of his Jewish roots, in his commitment to the underdog, and in his identification with the other, Jacobstein reveals a deep affinity with the older poet. "Pre-Med," for instance, displays the kind of unflinching investigation of pain and ferocious empathy we associate with Levine:

> "All semester in Psych Lab I shocked"
>
> the nictitating membrane of a white rabbit
> (every ten seconds for seven minutes).
> Our professor was making his name
> puréeing smart planaria and feeding them
> to dumb ones who then became smart.
> ...Deliver direct electrical current—
> *It's mild*, he assured us—to that opaque bit
> of ocular tissue, then enter the subjects'
> responses into the charts in our cross-hatched
> notebooks. I recall the experimenter (E—me)
> seemed upset, for more distressed
> that the subject (S: sleek fur, berry eyes),
> though in time E would master the art of labeling
> someone else's pain *a little discomfort.*

(6)

Similarly, in "Home Run," which describes how Jacobstein's father made french fries for the neighborhood kids, we find something like Levine's appreciation for simple people and simple pleasures. As his father cooks "the golden, hand-hewn fries, edges / beveled like cut gems,"

> ...Sweat pearls on his scalp:
>
> a windshield's first drops of rain,
> wiped away, returning. It's the sweat
>
> of running the bases, the ball rolling
> between left and center all the way
>
> to the fence. It's the good sweat of
> a good man: my father, headed home.
>
> (57)

One way in which Jacobstein's work differs from Levine's is in its frequent use of humor. Levine typically examines his subjects with the matter-of-fact ruthlessness of a county coroner. Jacobstein, in contrast, is often jokey, even about the possibility of dying. In "Bypass," he describes life's terrible swiftness this way:

> One day it's Miss Scarlet with
> the Candlestick in the Conservatory,
> the next they're carting someone
> down the corridor to where Dr. Black
> with the chisel in the O.R.
> waits to crack the vault of a chest.
>
> (36)

Unlike many writers of his generation, the generation that went to Vietnam and whose sense of "objectivity" and "legitimacy" were eroded by the culture shocks of the 60's and 70's, Jacobstein seems remarkably confident in his ability to tell a story. In a characteristic moment he says, "It all comes back to him in the cafeteria as he waits to vote," and he then proceeds to recreate a vintage 1960's Detroit high school cafeteria, complete with "Wonder Bread [to] squeegee the last streaks of gravy: thick, opaque, the exact faded yellow of Mr. Franzke's '58 Pontiac" (34). Similarly, Jacobstein's way of telling a story is very much his own. Moments and actions collide, coalesce, and explode in often unpredictable ways, full of emotional color, thereby creating an almost lyric narrative, as in the wonderful "Nuclear Family Vacation Blues," which recounts a car trip to the Southwest, "Anasazi ruins at Mesa Verde, atomic debris." The contrast between his mother trying to teach her two sons and the restless curiosity of the sons is quite exhilarating.

> Mom teaches Romance
> Languages, Spanish and French, throws in
> some Dante now and then. *Dante al dente*
> she calls it. *Esposa* means wife, yet *esposas*
> are handcuffs, see? But the boys want pinball
> not lessons in sexism…They love the shuffleboard,
> the swimming pools shaped like lima beans…
> though Vegas was OK, watching the fruits spin
> on the slots, the purple neon splitting the sky.
> And sometimes the road kill can be really cool.
>
> (32)

If Jacobstein has a weakness, it's that he sometimes pushes the humor too far. "Reincarnation," for instance, which begins on a playful note ("If they're right, this mosquito dive-bombing my ear / into total *presence* at 3 A.M. is Rasputin, or your late / Schnauzer"), continues ever more fancifully, working hard to make something of the subject until finally at the very end, it uncovers something deeper: "someone's / cousin or mother or child circles overhead / / in her newfound brown body, shaking the last / of her human tears from her glistening wings…" (43).

One also finds occasionally flat or fatigued language. Those french fries, for instance, "always taste like luck." On the evidence of this book, which, after all, is only his first full-length effort, Jacobstein's forte is not the clever metaphor, but a sense of real life anchored in the language of history and science. In "Near Rusomo," a poem about the Rwanda genocide which recalls Carolyn Forché's "The Colonel," he shows us the bodies of victims floating in the Kagera River:

> And now
> that the machetes have passed,
> the torsos are looking down
> into the debris-choked shallows
> for their missing heads and limbs.
>
> (16)

At its best, *Ripe* is a work of considerable maturity, and offers us not just good stories and good laughs, but also a compassionate vision of our common suffering and joys.

kari edwards

I TRY TO AVOID THE VOID ALTOGETHER

my ashen words hang on my side with no particular categories, forced into split level idioms. I used the wrong ones in keyholes and ordered a self issue subscription of myself to myself. I know I am without tax, or text, or a real development plans, just some cracked glass and a chocolate grinder with its own dual site of "I'm not it," "seek only when I want to." and as far as pornography, I just replace the pronouns and nouns: she for he for she, dog for a child for grandma for a loaded revolver, warm and trustworthy—a fragment or example that gets reprinted just before extinction. distribution is widespread to the obvious misplaced positions between the bed and refrigerator…I mean greatest hits album and…no, it's already tuesday, which is different than most four letter words, but with the same post arrangement of incidents—full of whistle stops and padded knees.

kari edwards

STUFF ON NAMES

liquid burns away a hard morning dust
a single syllable of permissible lies count's bodies and change

objects in walls
talking heads and slippery tongues

a slight of hand and puff of smoke dazzles us
engulfs our ignorance in hermit crab resilience

a doors shut
lips are sealed

either you're part of the song
or accumulating benefits for the dead

the method is progress
the foliage plastic

a letter is written
ashes returned

the label says
reread instructions / failed inspection

another calls: "I am going to kill myself…?
"we have an opening next Tuesday at 10:00 A.M."

Roger Fanning

ROAD TRIP

"There isn't a line in the world," someone
once said. And Paul Klee rightly claimed

that "drawing and writing are fundamentally
identical." And Cindy Crawford cherishes

her mole. Her agent pressured her
to have it removed, but Cindy

drew the line, figuratively speaking (literally,
she ended with a dot), whereas a cartographer

traffics in actual lines (dots too), omitting maybe
a cul-de-sac, maybe a toxic creek. He makes

a mistake to wink at the way things really are, so
his work can then be copyrighted—sold—

because cartography, like Cindy Crawford
sanctifying her mole, is ultimately a practical art.

Was Zeno being practical when he supposed
a line is made up of an infinite number of points?

No, but Roethke was: "Lust fatigues the soul."
Also Mishima: "Lust inevitably

attaches itself to fragments." So if
you've driven all day, pondering trade-

and beauty marks and map minutiae
and Andy Warhol's soup cans and the endless

implications of mass production, it's then
that the blue blue information signs

positively sing of GAS FOOD LODGING
and you feel invisible, enchanted, lost:

flawless, so to speak.

Geoffrey Gatza

HOW TO TELL IF YOUR POETRY IS CHOKING

If you observe "conscious" Poetry choking:

—Ask, "Are you choking?"

—If the poet can speak, cough, or breathe, DO NOT INTERFERE.

—If the poet CANNOT speak, cough, or breathe, give sub-diaphragmatic abdominal thrusts (*the Mainstream maneuver*) until the foreign body is expelled or the poet becomes unconscious. (*Or in case of extreme obesity or late pregnancy, give chest thrusts.*)

—Be persistent.

—Continue uninterrupted until the obstruction is relieved or advanced life support is available. In either case the poet should be examined by a physician as soon as possible.

PREVENTION IS NO ACCIDENT

To perform the Mainstream maneuver, the following steps should quickly be taken:

- Stand behind the poet who is choking.

- Place your arms around their waist and get them to bend forward at the waist.

- Clench one hand into a fist and place it over the person's belly button, or navel.

- Place the opposite hand on top of the first.

- Thrust both hands at the same time backward into the stomach with a hard, upward movement. In those who are extremely obese or pregnant, the hands should be centered over the person's chest and chest thrusts should be given instead of stomach thrusts.

- Repeat the thrusting movements every few seconds until the object in the person's windpipe is coughed up and expelled from their mouth. The Mainstream maneuver should also be stopped if the person becomes unconscious.

Gary Sullivan

HOW MAINSTREAM IS IT?

It's not enough that we should succeed: Everyone else must fail. We want ads EVERYWHERE: It's not enough that Linford Christie once wore the Puma logo on his Contact lenses. Or that "we" served in Vietnam, the Gulf War Neither is it "enough" that we're the most environmentally Contaminated place in the Western Hemisphere, nor that We pick apart everything Tiger Woods does on the Golf Course. It's just not enough to go around weepy and confused.

A "for instance": Mr. Potato Head's naked & fellating Tiger Woods. Is that enough? Every year 1000s of mice, rats and guinea pigs Are injected with chemicals to see if they do actual damage to Organs. That's why we have to be witnesses. It's not That we *personally* have experienced forgiveness of sin. The hoi polloi require creators re-invent themselves & that we routinely lead them w/the tools and processes we have.

And they have to PAY FOR the writing, the EU haircuts Otherwise, people simply turn away from us & we are Neither too good nor too bad & are simply recycled—Pardon? What do you mean, "Is that not enough"? You might as well ask, "Is it enough that the shower heads in The women's locker room are at chin-height, that Our poems are endlessly overacted, tirelessly over-emotive & pedantically... melodramatically...morbidly contrived?"

If everyone's going to be like that, the stadium must be named after Some stupid product: "The Ban on Meat-based Feeds," "After September 11," "Grandstanding & Witless Protest Signs." It's not enough that they invite us into their homes, to "live in Texas" with them. The key word here is "constantly." Must we constantly start over? Are we any closer to God? Why must we constantly prove ourselves? Must we constantly Be on guard against those "experts" who seem to think we are Totally inept and idiotic by virtue of being sheepish?

Human Destiny tells us that, just as we fashion laws to meet our Emerging needs, so must we constantly reexamine and revise Our poetry, and that our poetry not be at war with our "customers." We simply can't depend on the same individuals year after year To do the work. Poetry is too often used to solve specific Applied problems. Why must we constantly build new functions?

Have we not hearts big enough? Must we constantly revert to the Eighteenth century or, preferably, the seventeenth? Is *that* why we intoxicate ourselves? Distract ourselves? Constantly bombard each other with crap? Why must we Pit ourselves *against* crap? Does crap prevent us from seeing "The Big Picture"?

Can't we learn to enjoy the simple pleasures of helicopter noise? Must we constantly compare our helicopters to Other helicopters? Why must we constantly theorize about helicopters? Are they an appropriate code for living? Are they even "Realistic"?

We talk as if thought was precise and emotion was vague As if thought were a function of understanding As if there were no hand there to guide the scalpel's cutting As if thought were something "plunged into a sea of words & come up dripping." Do thoughts even work? Thought ought To be the most democratic of arenas, but has become Just another obscure professional specialty, the corpse wheeled away, The kidneys, the glands, the bruised heart—all tossed into a saucepan.

As poets, we need to embody wisdom, dignity, freedom & love Helping others to own these values, to reach the point Where they are ready to embark on their own lives, free of social roles. We need to embody regeneration through the synergy of Expressive breath, sound and movement. We need to transform What we are restoring, and to ask these questions with great Patience and intention, to embody them, to live them & to support programs that foster great patience and intention.

RIGHT NOW is an extremely important time for the "Core Self." We need to embody the whole of our human nature To devise systems of rules (selves) which describe how language Works; we need to embody—to give birth to—all of our "selves." We have many selves: the image (fantasy/memory/dream) self, The physical self, the soul. It's time [APPLAUSE]. With this in mind, we can better prepare ourselves for the future Adopt policies of dignity, inclusion, and fair treatment [APPLAUSE].

Each self is different [APPLAUSE]. They are each different & we need to embody those values in our new laws [APPLAUSE]. If hope is going to be more than a theological theory, we need to Embody, in the dramatic pattern each of us of calls, "my life," These values *as* legislation, because the court will not do it For us [APPLAUSE]. We need to embody choreographers [APPLAUSE] so that way we may understand the world more in "human" terms. We think that is the point. For you and I to live an effective life We need to embody successful consumer driven initiatives (principles) So as to "get" a grasp of the kinds of connections and relations between Things. [APPLAUSE.]

August Highland

MAYBE NOT

i am gaining weight every year
this is unlikely to be a terrorist act

today someone knocked their cart into me at costco
this is unlikely to be a terrorist act

every year my hair is graying at the sideburns
this is unlikely to be a terrorist act

my mother-in-law is a creep
this is unlikely to be a terrorist act

i picked a bad watermelon at the store
and i was positive i had picked a ripe one
this is unlikely to be a terrorist act

my own mother is beginning to show genuine affection
toward me for the first time in my life
this is unlikely to be a terrorist act

a girl half my age flirted with me at starbucks
this is unlikely to be a terrorist act

i am a very giving person and sometimes people
take advantage of me
this is unlikely to be a terrorist act

people often mistake me for being gay
this is unlikely to be a terrorist act

i have never had a threesome but my wife has
this is unlikely to be a terrorist act

my cat died recently at the age of 17
this is unlikely to be a terrorist act

i am going to die one day
this is unlikely to be a terrorist act

Rosmarie Waldrop

RELATIONAL ASPECTS

First research. Parents, trees ravaged with hunger. (Erotic?) If I feel anonymous, is the infinite unsexed? If my name is, does anyone know why? Smell like a healthy unwashed child. Words used over and over to cover an emotional impasse. Under wet eyes.

Anxiety interwoven with the fact of life, impersonal as machinery, sandwiches and spilled beer. Confirmed by travel. How to unravel affective cause without unraveling myself.

A kingdom of caresses remembered with such clarity it must be false. The cat's serene madness. As opposed to communication.

Under the cold eye of mother or mirror secret structures are laid bare. What if there is no image? No gypsies out of the woods? All verb without subject? Learning to read timetables or growing tall out of a shell?

Into the flowing world. Not push but leap. Not pull but peal. Of laughter? Sponged up by perspective. Aggressive impulses or chronic clumsiness? More clearly defined at the bend in the road.

A new integration reveals a notebook. Filled with a web of sins to snare the priest. His attention was stuck on counting to ten.

The more magical the letters. Rays of light break up inside the oracle. And divide into a paradisal spectrum continues into its own shadow.

Beyond the end of the line. Along tarred roads. Not lawns or croquet. I played with lithograph stones in back of the printshop.

Nakedness misled into promiscuities of language. The countryside unastonished rather than cool valley. If the limits of the mind expand without attaining orgasm the girl ages on a plateau of gesture. Eating her heart out like everybody else.

Alan Sondheim

MY COMPOSITION IN LANGUAGE

It is entirely irrelevant to the world whether we exist or not.

Nothing is relevant to the world.

Existential statements serve an evolutionary purpose, the reification of the self.

What occurs in language in relation to the copula or self-reflexivity, has no effect whatsoever on the world.

Nothing has any effect whatsoever on the world.

Self-reflexive recognition is a form of pointing-out or gesture, in the guise of naming (by virtue of nominalism).

Consciousness, self-consciousness, is a defense mechanism.

There is nothing to 'it' beyond this.

It is a mistake to assume that consciousness exists outside of language.

It resides in language; it is a tool which occupies or declares nothing.

Declaration occurs only in language. Physical gesture cleaves the air.

Inscriptions transform the imminent world of the substrate.

An effect already exhausts.

Culture is built on the predication that language means, and therefore acts and creates.

Words are nothing and do nothing. The performative is a contextual myth.

Alarum is spread by language, just as identity precedes language.

"In its early stages the ballet also yielded ornaments which moved kaleidoscopically, But even after they had discarded their ritual meaning, they remained still the plastic formation of the erotic life which gave rise to them and determined their traits." (Kracauer)

We speak to ourselves. We speak for ourselves.

We never speak. Language has never been employed.'

The self-reflexivity of language is the routing of resonance; all objects and cultures are resonant holdfasts for our existence.

Neither objects nor cultures exist.

"The cornered vessel (ku) has no longer corners. What a 'cornered' vessel! What a 'cornered' vessel!" (Confucius)

The ku has never existed.

Language infiltrates speaker, spoken, and spoken-to with its semantic skein. Likewise, the skein does not exist.

Speaking, spoken, and spoken-to, are correlated actions in the world.

They have no relevance.

The correlation is nearly decomposable. Every speaking is a composition. Every composition is an appearance. Every appearance is an illusion.

Illusions are subject to entropy and dissolution. Neither the appearance nor the illusion exists. What does not exist, disseminates, dissembles, dissimulates.

Our existence is an illusion.

The world is neither an illusion nor a copula. The world is all that is neither an illusion nor a copula.

Nothing is relevant to the world. The world is nothing.

Alan Sondheim

MY COMPOSITION2 IN LANGUAGE

It is entirely irrelevant to the world whether we exist or not. It is entirely relevant to us.

Nothing is relevant to the world. The world would not exist without us.

Existential statements serve an evolutionary purpose, the reification of the self. Existential statements procure the world in relation to our perception.

What occurs in language in relation to the copula or self-reflexivity, has no effect whatsoever on the world. The world transforms with each and every utterance.

Nothing has any effect whatsoever on the world. There is no 'world,' only a confluence of interrelated protocols and effects.

Self-reflexive recognition is a form of pointing-out or gesture, in the guise of naming (by virtue of nominalism). Pointing-out symbolizes the recognition which takes place all the way back, beginning with retinal learning; the pointing-out is a consensus or coherency for others, for community.

Consciousness, self-consciousness, is a defense mechanism. Consciousness defines and procures thought.

There is nothing to 'it' beyond this. It is entirely beyond this, beyond this and others, beyond community and communality.

It is a mistake to assume that consciousness exists outside of language. Consciousness is a priori and comes with the first imminence of the world.

It resides in language; it is a tool which occupies or declares nothing. Consciousness declares everything, internal or external to language.

Declaration occurs only in language. Physical gesture cleaves the air. Declaration is always prior to language; gesture cleaves thought itself, the psychogeographical substrate of the world.

Inscriptions transform the imminent world of the substrate. Inscriptions are contiguous to the substrate at best.

An effect already exhausts. An effect is always new; nothing repeats.

Culture is built on the predication that language means, and therefore acts and creates. Language is build on the predication of the dialect between body and environment; culture creates, and language follows.

Words are nothing and do nothing. The performative is a contextual myth. Words are everything; every utterance is an active performative. The world becomes comprehension and comprehends through language.

Alarum is spread by language, just as identity precedes language. Language comforts and transforms house into home; identity is situated in language, just as alarum is subdued.

"In its early stages the ballet also yielded ornaments which moved kaleidoscopically, But even after they had discarded their ritual meaning, they remained still the plastic formation of the erotic life which gave rise to them and determined their traits." (Kracauer)

We speak to ourselves. We speak for ourselves. We speak only to others. We speak only for them. This is the erotic gesture of culture.

We never speak. Language has never been 'employed.' We always speak; language always employs the other as our master.

The self-reflexivity of language is the routing of resonance; all objects and cultures are resonant holdfasts for our existence. Nothing depends on language, which derails the resonance of the world.

Neither objects nor cultures exist. Objects and cultures exist in spite of ourselves, others, and the symbolic resolution of language.

"The cornered vessel (ku) has no longer corners. What a 'cornered' vessel! What a 'cornered' vessel!" (Confucius)

The ku has never existed. The ku has always existed; it is Confucius who has disappeared.

Language infiltrates speaker, spoken, and spoken-to with its semantic skein. Likewise, the skein does not exist. Language deludes the speaking of the body; the skein of culture exists a priori to language. The sememe itself is a priori.

Speaking, spoken, and spoken-to, are correlated actions in the world. Speaking, spoken, and spoken-to, are mutually incoherent; they signify the breaking of the world, the tendency towards dissolution. What they hold, is released; what they confine, is loosened.

They have no relevance. They are relevant; it is their byproduct and phenomenology, their glance, that describes everything.

The correlation is nearly decomposable. Every speaking is a composition. Every composition is an appearance. Every appearance is an illusion. The correlation falls to pieces. Every speaking breaks with self, world, and others. Every breaking is immeasurable. Every breaking alludes.

Illusions are subject to entropy and dissolution. Neither the appearance nor the illusion exists. What does not exist, disseminates, dissembles, dissimulates. Speaking is subject to joining. Speaking, by measure of its breaking, is substrate to appearance. What disseminates, dissembles, dissimulates, returns, assembles, seminates, within the broken of language.

Our existence is an illusion. Our existence is the only real.

The world is neither an illusion nor a copula. The world is all that is neither an illusion nor a copula. The world coheres through the breaking of the copula.

Nothing is relevant to the world. The world is nothing. Everything is relevant; the world is everything. The relevance of the world is the beginning of politics.

Alan Sondheim

MY LAST COMPOSITION OF LANGUAGE

It is entirely irrelevant to the world whether we exist or not. It is entirely relevant to us. It is irrelevant to us whether we exist or not; that is the truth to be learned.

Nothing is relevant to the world. The world would not exist without us. We would not exist without the world; we do not exist.

Existential statements serve an evolutionary purpose, the reification of the self. Existential statements procure the world in relation to our perception. Existential statements are a priori errors in relation to the world. They disguise our truth and the truth of the world.

What occurs in language in relation to the copula or self-reflexivity, has no effect whatsoever on the world. The world transforms with each and every utterance. There is neither transformation nor non-transformation. The world is an illusion of its truth.

Nothing has any effect whatsoever on the world. There is no 'world,' only a confluence of interrelated protocols and effects. There is world and non-world; we are ghosts looking in at the world; we are ghosts looking at ourselves. To eliminate perception of ourselves and the world is the truth of ourselves and the world. To see ourselves by not-seeing ourselves as ghosts, that is the truth of the world.

Self-reflexive recognition is a form of pointing-out or gesture, in the guise of naming (by virtue of nominalism). Pointing-out symbolizes the recognition which takes place all the way back, beginning with retinal learning; the pointing-out is a consensus or coherency for others, for community. Pointing out collapses the world, just as nourishment and sleep collapses the world. To eliminate the learning before language, to eliminate language, that is the truth of the world.

Consciousness, self-consciousness, is a defense mechanism. Consciousness defines and procures thought. Consciousness and self-conscious break in relation to the world; through the broken, light emerges, that is the truth of the world.

There is nothing to 'it' beyond this. 'It' is entirely beyond this, beyond this and others, beyond community and communality. 'It' is already an error of perception; forget 'it' and the truth of the world emerges.

It is a mistake to assume that consciousness exists outside of language. Consciousness is a priori and comes with the first imminence of the world. Immanence is neither of consciousness nor the world; nor is immanence of language or the a prior, that is the truth of the world.

It resides in language; it is a tool which occupies or declares nothing. Consciousness declares everything, internal or external to language. There is nothing to declare, nothing to emerge. Declaration is false existence, non-declaration is false existence.

Declaration occurs only in language. Physical gesture cleaves the air. Declaration is always prior to language; gesture cleaves thought itself, the psychogeographical substrate of the world. Declaration occurs everywhere among gestures. Gestures declare; the world emerges without declaration, that is the truth of the world.

Inscriptions transform the imminent world of the substrate. Inscriptions are contiguous to the substrate at best. Inscriptions are the substrate which must be comprehended to be forgotten; that is the emergence of the world.

An effect already exhausts. An effect is always new; nothing repeats. An effect has no being, no relevance, that is the truth of the world.

Culture is built on the predication that language means, and therefore acts and creates. Language is build on the predication of the dialectic between body and environment; culture creates, and language follows. Following or leading make no difference; what goes before, goes behind.

Words are nothing and do nothing. The performative is a contextual myth. Words are everything; every utterance is an active performative. The world becomes comprehension and comprehends through language. The becoming of the world is not the world, and the comprehension of the world is not the comprehension of the world. Everything and nothing are nothing and everything, that is the truth of the world.

Alarum is spread by language, just as identity precedes language. Language comforts and transforms house into home; identity is situated in language, just as alarum is subdued. Alarum for what, alarum hinders, ties one to oneself, to the languaging and things of the world. Alarum ties one to identity, identity ties one to language, to the world. Break identity and alarum, that is the truth of the world.

"In its early stages the ballet also yielded ornaments which moved kaleidoscopically, But even after they had discarded their ritual meaning, they remained still the plastic formation of the erotic life which gave rise to them and determined their traits." (Kracauer)

We speak to ourselves. We speak for ourselves. We speak only to others. We speak only for them. This is the erotic gesture of culture. Speaking and eroticism tie one to broken meaning, taken for the meaning of truth, for the truth of meaning. Break what is already broken, that is the truth of the world. Do not break what is already broken, that is the truth of the world.

We never speak. Language has never been 'employed.' We always speak; language always employs the other as our master. Speaking negates the world; speaking is always busy. In silence is the world's truth, after employment and non-employment.

The self-reflexivity of language is the routing of resonance; all objects and cultures are resonant holdfasts for our existence. Nothing depends on language, which derails the resonance of the world. Dependency and resonance, already an investment; eliminate dependency and resonance, eliminate investment, that is the truth of the world.

Neither objects nor cultures exist. Objects and cultures exist in spite of ourselves, others, and the symbolic resolution of language. More hindrance! more hindrance!

"The cornered vessel (ku) has no longer corners. What a 'cornered' vessel! What a 'cornered' vessel!" (Confucius)

The ku has never existed. The ku has always existed; it is Confucius who has disappeared. Confucius exists and does not exist; the ku exists and does not exist. So many objects! Forget existence and non-existence, that is the truth of the world.

Language infiltrates speaker, spoken, and spoken-to with its semantic skein. Likewise, the skein does not exist. Language deludes the speaking of the body; the skein of culture exists a priori to language. The sememe itself is a priori. Skein and sememe, all these structures; what else emerges? What emerges, does not emerge; what does not emerge, emerges. Forget emerging, in silence, that is the truth of the world.

Speaking, spoken, and spoken-to, are correlated actions in the world. Speaking, spoken, and spoken-to, are mutually incoherent; they signify the breaking of the world, the tendency towards dissolution. What they hold, is released; what they confine, is loosened. Coherency is the skein of the self; non-coherency is the skein of the world. Coherency and non-coherency are joined by others and the spoken-to. The world fragments among the assumption of contraries, divisions, typifications. Forget coherency; the world coheres. Forget non-coherency; the world falls apart.

They have no relevance. They are relevant; it is their byproduct and phenomenology, their glance, that describes everything. The description of everything is the falsehood of the world; the truth of the world is neither description nor non-description.

The correlation is nearly decomposable. Every speaking is a composition. Every composition is an appearance. Every appearance is an illusion. The correlation falls to pieces. Every speaking breaks with self, world, and others. Every breaking is immeasurable. Every breaking alludes. Breaking interferes; what is broken, has edges; what has edges, longs for completion. Forget composition and decomposition; be a ghost! Illusion and reality, all the same, that is the truth of the world.

Illusions are subject to entropy and dissolution. Neither the appearance nor the illusion exists. What does not exist, disseminates, dissembles, dissimulates. Speaking is subject to joining. Speaking, by measure of its breaking, is substrate to appearance. What disseminates, dissembles, dissimulates, returns, assembles, seminates, within the broken of language. Breaking and coming together, as of the spheres, that is nothing. Semination and dissemination, that is nothing but the seduction of the symbolic. Forget stasis and process, entropy and non-entropy, equilibrium and non-equilibrium, they are naming, and naming is not the province of ghosts. Be a ghost, that is the truth of the world.

Our existence is an illusion. Our existence is the only real. Our existence is our non-existence; our illusion is our real; our real is our illusion, our non-existence is our existence. Be a ghost, that is the truth of the world.

The world is neither an illusion nor a copula. The world is all that is neither an illusion nor a copula. The world coheres through the breaking of the copula. There is no copula without division, a white horse is not a horse, pairs never unite, that is the truth of the world.

Nothing is relevant to the world. The world is nothing. Everything is relevant; the world is everything. The relevance of the world is the beginning of politics. The beginning of politics is the end of politics; the world is neither relevant nor irrelevant, nothing or everything. Be a ghost! That is the truth of the world, be a ghost!

Thomas Lux

GUIDE TO THE PERPETUALLY PERPLEXED

Don't hurt your brain on this: if the arrow points left
it's left you should go. Then
take your first right,
then the next right,
again the next right and *then*
a left. If you head-on a cement truck
then it is as it should be. Too much
perplexity and soon everyone's head
is a revolving hologram of a question mark!
Instead: if the sign says USE YOUR WORDS,
then use your words,
in this order: subject, verb, object.
Instead: if the sign says SHUT THE FUCK UP
then you should shut the fuck up.
If it comes over the intercom to get in line,
for gosh sakes, then get in line, your wings
to the wall and eyes forward.
Do nothing to further perplex the other perplexed.
We'll let you know when it's single file for lunch
where it's first your place-mats
of puzzles and impossible dots to disconnect
followed by your beans, and your brown meat, gray,
over which you'll pray, oh yes, you'll pray,
if you don't want us to break your neck.

Tom Clark

FALLOUT

Under cold stars of winter, hard points of light
Shine as expressionlessly as the eyes of the dead.

In Connecticut and Nebraska, wind sings in frozen power lines.
In Ohio, cars have been abandoned up to their windows in drifts,

Bright roofs shining in the sidelong glancing of the distant
Sun like glistening outer bodies of insects in transformation.

Over the Great Slave Lake heaven opens up and down floats irradiated
Metal, a shimmering light descending, iridescent plankton aglow

In slow flakes. It's some kind of exercise. The war,
We know, is over. Still, "What's out there?" people ask,

"Are we alone?"

Tom Clark

THE VACANT ESTATE

The estate stands vacant: the silent stone dogs,
The lawns well grassed, the checkered polyanthus,
The polished porphyry, and—thus
The fool's delusion of an opening—
All the machines are running. It appears
They have simply turned them on and gone.
The coral root oozes syrup sharp as quince,
Jasmine clings to the perspiring palms,
By the rock silverlings glide belly up.
In your dream all the machines are running
(Can they be turned off?) out of the empty house
Across the emerald turf toward you,
Tridents waving like wild stalks of corn,
Antennae scraping the clouds…and then they're gone.
You turn around and it's tomorrow,
Nature has shut her doors.

Adam Clay

BLIND ALPHABET: I

After The Months of Little Sleep,
Marian learned all the words
Stitched like string
In the English tongue.
Her favorites are written on her thighs and sleeves:
Brine, flux, furl, fjord.
She wonders where the messenger swan songs
Have gone.
Her head hungers for the belly's emptiness.
The words are like wolves
Tearing the torsos of curtain trees.
The words are like wolves
Sucking wind from the river,
Spilling blood into the smutched air.

Gerald Locklin

GEORGES BRAQUE: *ARTIST AND MODEL,* 1939

always the moralist,
he is transforming eve
into geometry,
her midriff into the
shroud of turin.

but swaddled hips
will not allow us to forget
the delta of our simmering,

and everlasting electricity
will once again be triggered by
the tiniest of mammary electrodes,

as creativity and procreation
once more coincide.

Harry Nudel

AFTER...

apres la guerre
tra la la

apres la tra
la la

apres guere
la la

apres la la

apres la

apres

tra la la tra...

Halvard Johnson

SOMEWHERE AROUND BARSTOW

The Iranian assured us that all spent fuel would be returned to Russia. The Visitor's Center was closed, so we had to go on without maps, without guidance. The media tried to fill the emptiness within us, but even the launching of moon orbiters

failed to do the trick. We thought we'd settled on a political blueprint for our nation's future, but even that didn't pan out, though a conference hall full of astrophysicists had worked on it day and night for several weeks. Either the surface had been dried

out by solar heating and maturation, or the dark soot-like material that covers Barstow's surface masked any trace of Arizona black ice. But still the road uncoiled before us until we surpassed it and it slithered away behind us in our rear-view mirror. The boundaries between counties hereabouts

were not well marked, and we usually slid from one right into the next without warning, tours no longer being offered until further notice. The Humans in Space Symposium had been cancelled, stirring up a hornet's nest of activity among those impacted.

In Arroyo City, we stopped to gas up, and to check out Arizona's claim that it had no nuclear or biological weapons programs, a claim we strongly doubted. Now that we pay at the pump, we never see any of the locals anymore, and everything else was underground

except, of course, for the old, burnt-out roadhouse across the road from the pumps. Hand in hand, a column of kindergarten children marched by us, headed out along the road we'd followed into town, vanishing into the heat vapors rising from the pavement

and the desert floor. Where they were headed we had no idea. Our newly bolstered inspection team visited a former nuclear facility forty-six miles south of Flagstaff. This, I thought, is eternity. A policeman biking past smiled, "The ball's in the bad guy's court now."

Eleanor Wilner

JUST SO STORY

"Do Not Make Treaties with These People"
—translation of Navajo message inscribed
on the disk left on the moon by NASA

It is very quiet on the moon. A cat squarls—
but that is back on earth, on streets of stone
where sound echoes: trashcans tipped over,
glass breaking, fear in a gray overcoat firing its
guns; it is all metal on metal—a plumber's snake
trying to shed its iron skin, clanking, sparks
flying; a steel beak hatching out of an egg
of glass, the cracking shell a shatter of ice
in the ear. While on the moon, an airless peace:
the craters aglow with distant sun, and nothing
to disturb the quiet dust.
                              In a grove deep in the past,
when the ibex was still bidden by its image drawn
with a stick in the sand—a lion came down to drink
where the moon lay, white and naked, on the pond,
trails of light around her, a corona of snakes.
The lion was very thirsty, and it drank and drank,
until the pond was dry, and the moon the barest
glimmer on the mud. And that is how darkness
first escaped from the place it had lain
on the bottom of the pond.
                              Now, the blood
from the kill no longer returns to the gods
so nothing is lost, but spills
in the road for the jackals to drink.
In the silence of the moon, Old Glory forever
flies in its fixed imitation of a flag in wind,
a permanent wave that can't disappoint

the eager cameras of the press by hanging limp
in the airless atmosphere of conquered space.
Far below, the busy cameras snap the photo-op:
a President, drawing his brows together
in the fixed imitation of a mind at work.
Down all the streets nearby, the wind rips
at the trash, you can hear the sound of
shredders in the shuttered rooms. Dogs bark.
The subway shakes the sidewalk grates.
Everywhere, the dark ascends
by stairs, by escalators, up through manholes
with their covers pushed away. Even by day,
though just a bit more slowly, the dark extends
its sway. The rats are growing bolder now;
you can hear the steady sound of gnawing
where they have dragged the last bright crust
of moon into their hole.

Jesse Waters

THE PROBLEM WITH CRUMBS

Sisters get hungry.

The sylvan floor is damp.

A hint of yeast attracts insects.

Birds can see even seeds from great heights.

Gingerbread smells so good in the wrong forest,

that smell can make your brother forget his own careful pattern—

might make your parents throw you out like day-old bread.

Jesse Waters

SWINE LOGIC

In the time of pigs and wolves
and the regularity of speaking

creatures wrought with instinct
and the taste for blood,

I'd have thought like pigs;
I, too, would've believed in the progression

of what seemed safe. When all you've ever known
are fields of mud, some black straw laced

straight and patched with your own shit seems
like it will hold you and your siblings tight—

then some bad ass blows the whole deal down.
So you go to wrist-thick sticks—same deal—then bricks;

A thumb print over your x-rayed heart.
Feeling the phone might ring, or go quiet forever.

A story with its lesson in metastasis,
Death, in a wolf's baptismal breath: huff, huff, huff.

The world outside begins its howl of hope against you;
you play sincere Pinochle with kin in candle-shadows, confident…

Catherine Daly

REVIEW:
UNRAVELING AT THE NAME by JENNY FACTOR
Copper Canyon, 2001. $14.00

The poems in Jenny Factor's first book are special since at every level they illuminate cultural constructs using poetical constructs. The use of traditional form in poetry, as in these poems, illustrates not only the way in which language use and realism are complicated by traditional form, but also the ways in which cultural constructs complicate women's experience.

While nominalism marks even realist poetry, women's poetry may be considered to move between abstraction and realism somewhat differently than men's poetry, especially if one considers women to participate somewhat differently than men participate in culturally-mediated ideas of "reality" and "ideation." Factor focuses her poetry where physical and cultural differences are most acute: sex, childbearing, and marriage. Additionally, since until very recently a woman's name changes at least one during her lifetime, the nouns which identify female artists and thinkers are unstable. Factor points to this double naming, the poet naming reality and idea, the culture naming the woman, in her title, *Unraveling at the Name*. The title also serves as a trope for her content, since her content is the way in which she correlates experience and language.

Marilyn Hacker, judge of the Hayden Carruth Award the year Factor won it, is the leading Jewish lesbian feminist formalist poet in English; Hacker was an important exemplar and mentor to Factor even before Hacker chose Factor for publication. The leading Jewish lesbian feminist *former* formalist poet is Adrienne Rich, who is, like Factor, a Harvard / Radcliffe graduate. While many radical feminist poets believe that forms developed and "best" applied by men twist women's experience, Factor uses these received forms to form or control her experience, to allow her to communicate parts of her experience in a rational way, and to encapsulate this emotion in a "made thing." The narrative relates a story which was surely traumatic:

immediately after the birth of her son, Factor discovered she was a lesbian; she and her husband subsequently divorced.

The title poem of the collection is a corona of sonnets, a sequence of linked sonnets. In the second sonnet of the title sequence, the name has been is stitched by an unknown person on sheets, either like a monogram or like a label for a laundry service: "under sheets stitched with my name / I played the day again" (23). It is important to note that no female craftsperson like, perhaps most famously, the "Aunt Jennifer" in Adrienne Rich's "Aunt Jennifer's Tigers" has stitched the name. Whereas sewing has been historically used in women's poetry to indicate attention to craft, or form, here, in this formal poem, the name and its placement are more important than its stitching. In one reading, perhaps the simplest, the sheets are the page, the name, a poem, and their meaning, memory. In the last poem in the corona, which gathers the repeated lines, this one has become, "slept in sheets with someone else's name" (30). This time, it is the name which is never "named." Since in the poem and throughout the collection, Factor foregrounds questions of identity and sexual definition, the name remains a label.

Beside memory and paper, the sheets are history (and "his story" since there is an implied "his name"), the poems are narrative stories, and both are all sorts of covering. The other characters in the sequence are known only by first name. The words are set in a particularly "woven" or raveled sonnet sequence: coronas are linked by a pattern of repeated sonnet first and last lines. Each line which is repeated is generally all derived from an initial "master" sonnet. Here, this cento-like sonnet is last. It gathers and reconstrues the linking lines. This fifteenth sonnet anticipates in form one of the tried and true techniques of reading lines which are repeated in free verse as a reduction of the overall intended meaning of a free verse poem: here, the ending "puns," doubled meanings, and lyric epiphanies *are* the repeated lines. Repeating the lines a third time allows Factor even more doubled meaning and lyric epiphany than usual, as in the line italicized for its last repetition, "*So this is how a woman feels*" and in the closing couplet:

My story's underneath this history.
Turn off the radio. I want to sing.

(30)

Her story is underneath the covers and underneath the "his story" of traditional form. She rejects Jack Spicer's poet-as-radio comparison to embrace the lyric nature of the sonnet. In this corona, not only the lines the form demands, but also details, characters, and phrases repeat and vary even within this larger repetitive structure. "I'll tell you stories honest as my name / and listen to yours…"(29) she writes in the fourteenth (and penultimate) sonnet, which shares details, such as a Bruce Springsteen song on the radio, with the second sonnet in the sequence. This fourteenth sonnet is the only one in the sequence addressed directly to the reader. There are several sonnet sequences in the book: "Conciliation" opens the book with a sequence of blank verse fourteen line poems (which nevertheless use a great deal of rhyme); the sonnets in "Extramarital…" have subtitles, as do the sonnets in "Solétudes," a series of stylistic studies; "Learning Stick" has a sonnet for each of a woman learning to drive stick shift with a male beloved, a female beloved, and by herself. Of the sequences, it is the corona—on its own, "corona" as a word, as an image—which has always seemed to be a particularly female, even cervical, sign of authority. ("Crown," the other name for this type of sonnet sequence and also a synonym for the word "corona," is also a term for that stage in labor when the top of the baby's head is visible through the vaginal opening.) That a corona be the title sequence to this book is particularly appropriate, for in the book, Factor is giving birth to her voice, female-identified sexuality, and self (not to mention her son).

Factor was trained in writing in form by a legendary prosody teacher, Myra Livingston, who wrote, wrote about, and taught formal children's poetry in Los Angeles. Factor dedicated the volume to Livingston's memory. Among Livingston's opinions, which led her to reject free verse, were that children prefer formal poetry, and that writing as a child does not indicate presence of writing talent. Factor's return to poetry after a hiatus of nearly a decade, her use of form, her identification of her voice with the song of the traditionally-formed lyric are returns to her earliest poetic education. While Factor attended writing workshops including Seamus Heaney's while at Harvard / Radcliffe, she did not write much for the period of late adolescence / very early adulthood this book covers. In this book, Factor seeks to reintegrate her early experiences, prosody among them, into her adult and new sexual understanding.

By integrating a story, a unified content controlled and presented by form, she sends many messages aside from those of patriarchy, tradition, and writing as a woman. She establishes authorial authority through her formal control over metonymy and consistency of syntax. The poems are sexy and about sex. They are funny, but never reduce to "light verse." While her poems' unitary style, voice, and tone are shared by recent academic poetry, their strength and uniqueness inheres in her uniquely personal experience with poetic and cultural forms.

Lewis LaCook

THE PARENTS OF THE DECEASED

We want sweetness in our houses, and
to sleep, despite the bellow of these
machines embedded in our most
sensitive rooms, whose sheets

flap emblazoned with the lead
stare of invasion. It's over there,
they tell me, blowing up and
simmering down, until even air

coats with corpses, and now this dance
of who owns what begins, falling down
when we insulate our living rooms against
the savor of burned skin, the sound

in every tone of conquest: we want their lives
to crumple, streak; we want to burn their skies.

Matthea Harvey

SHIVER & YOU HAVE WEATHER
Engine: ☑☐

In the aftermath of calculus
your toast fell butter side down.

Squirrels swarmed the lawns
in flight patterns. The hovercraft

helped the waves along. From
every corner there was perspective.

On the billboards the diamonds
were real, in the stores, only zirconia.

I cc'ed you. I let you know.
Sat down to write the Black Ice Memo.

Dinner would be meager &
reminiscent of next week's lunch.

So what if I sat on the sectional?
As always I was beside myself.

Matthea Harvey

I MAY AFTER LEAVING YOU WALK QUICKLY
OR EVEN RUN

I meant me in the general sense
When I said did you want me.

The Old World smoked in the fireplace.
Rain fell in a post-Romantic way.

Heads in the planets, toes tucked
under carpets, that's how we got our bodies

through. The drink we drank was cordial.
In a spoon, the ceiling fan whirled.

The translator made the sign
for twenty horses backing away

from a lump of sugar. Glum
was the woman in the ostrich feather hat.

Ronald Alexander

HIS FAVORITE

Tschiakovsky's Fifth: *Andante maestoso*. There's only a vibration, a whisper a rumble. *Pianissimo*. We sit in darkness at the rear of the balcony, among the purists, where the sound is crisp. The conductor and musicians in black and white are illuminated in a distant square, curves of cream and gold, a backdrop of towering pipes, lights arching the proscenium, the red velvet of the seats. The maestro makes a sudden stab with his baton, signaling transition to the coda. The motto theme is urgent now, no longer in the minor, but the major. The timpanist strikes his kettledrums with wooly mallets, trombonists cleave space, the conductor rises and crouches on the podium, swerving left, hovering over the strings, then twisting to point at the horns. But I turn to watch Albert, to see him: the olive burnish of his complexion, the curve of his eyelashes, the serious ridge of his brow. He places his hand on my arm, looks at me, raising his eyebrows. These are the final measures. *Fortissimo. Allegro vivace*. This is fate. The psychological reversal. He puts his mouth next to my ear and whispers. Defeat turning into triumph.

Gerald Yelle

OVIDIAN LOVE SONGS AND THEIR PLACE IN RADIO HISTORY

Should the spineless backslide lose all trace of its negative heritage

where would we be?

Maybe finding detractors unable to pin us would inspire us to vanish

leaving only our tongues flapping with pride.

What we need is a song we can bend to. When we crack we mend,

but we wouldn't even crack with the right kind of music. Every song falls

into one of two matched sets known as cornucopia and the void,

all the while unveiling dream taxonomies of spirited

knaves whose aching hearts hold true case histories,

"frauds so well conducted" only a fool would refuse to be moved.

Refusing doesn't work. Much like refusing to work. So here goes mine:

Whose love is a wire, drawn though ever smaller dies, freeing

Daphne from the laurel, *Jean d'Arc's* heart from the heretic pyre.

Should your well run dry I will wed you back to water.

Cornell Brellenthin

THE GARDEN OF BARD

Imagine it singing there, restored
to reasoning. How can that veined tree
disagree that a sea slug once embarked
from liquid to the eye of Chaucer?

Why wouldn't the edge of any indigo iris
crow out morning dreams,
announcing the sun whose heat
is heavier than feathers
daubed with ink?

Long before Sophocles
rattled the blind, we puzzled,
hunted, saw the hound beginnings,
heard the shots sink ever vigilant
as moths who serve the light.

From the onset,
she has been singing her own death song,
and we echo, asking her to die,
assassins amazed at how quickly
the universe picks up the fallen
orange and places it back on the tree.

K. Silem Mohammad

ESSAY: SOUGHT POEMS

One of the signature characteristics of contemporary experimental poetry is its emphasis on procedures in which the poet's textual material is supplied at least in part before the act of composition as such begins: examples would include chance operations performed on source texts a la John Cage's "Writing through the Cantos" and Jackson Mac Low's *Stanzas for Iris Lezak*; Burroughsian "cut-up" exercises like those performed by Ted Berrigan in *The Sonnets*; other forms of collage such as Ronald Johnson's sampling of Milton in *RADI OS*; and homophonic translations in the manner of Louis Zukofsky's *Catullus* and David Melnick's *Men in Aïda*. Surrealist, Dadaism, Oulipo, and other avant-grade traditions, which have in turn exerted a heavy influence on New York School, Language, and subsequent experimentalist practice, have often used these methods in combination with some form of collaboration, further diffusing the role of the unitary author in rearranging and reimagining the source material.

I want to talk about a trend I see as particularly visible in recent work by certain post-avant poets, in which the collaborative element is supplied not necessarily by actual multiple authorship in the familiar sense (though this may happen as well), but by *simulated* multiple authorship, an enforced or feigned collaboration with other subjects— subjects whose real identities may even be unknown or untraceable. The process might seem to involve a kind of wholesale co-opting of individual voices, but these are voices which have already been co-opted or dis-opted many times over as a result of their insertion into the great random catalog of the internet, where their often intensely motivated messages are reproduced ad infinitum in instances of sublimely unmotivated chatter. In the extreme democracy of webspace, right-wing hate groups become bunkmates with Marxist ideologues, home-repair specialists, and lonely pet-owners, and their discourses sometimes form unlikely chemical reactions in such close proximity to one another. These imaginary fusions supply the raw ingredients for the *sought poem.*

"Sought poem," as opposed to "found poem"—or not so much *opposed to* as *extrapolated from.* Whereas the idea behind found poems is that they're just something you stumble upon and say hey, that's poetry, I'm thinking of a process of aggressively *looking* for something, with the intent of *enlisting* it in some capacity. Sought poems come about as the result of invasive surgeries performed on already-mangled bodies. The poet knows those happy—or unhappy, as the case may be—accidents of language are out there, but it may take repeated sallies into the underbrush before they are flushed out. The sought poem is not passively awaited, but teased, prodded, and hectored into existence. The poet thus assumes a level of involvement that in many ways is very old-school: she once again puts her manipulative ego into full gear, and becomes responsible for aggressively intentional structures. The intentions in question, however, are by necessity largely confined to the level of formal arrangement and sonic or visual style, leaving the field wide open for the accidents of theme that make the aesthetic flourishes possible in the first place.

For me the preferred medium has been the Google search engine, or rather the pages of search results that Google throws up. The typical process—one that I stole from Gary Sullivan, Father of "Flarf"—goes as follows. First, I enter some combination of search words and/or phrases: let's say "shock," "awe," "reindeer," and "peace sign." This gives me six results (with colored headers which can't be duplicated here because of the limitations of print):

Money Clips and Jewelry Designed by Skystone and Silver
... Rebel Flag Moneyclip Red Panda Earrings Red Panda Pendant **Reindeer** Pendant
Road Bombs Pendant 3rd Army Pendant 7th Cavalry Pendant **Shock** & **Awe** Pendant. ...
www.skystoneandsilver.com/store.html - 75k - Mar 28, 2003 - Cached - Similar pages

Sailor Moon S Movie
...is actually a blimp carrying a sleigh with blow-up **reindeer** in front....Luna watches
on in **awe** and blushes slightly ... Usagi has a look of **shock** on her face which is ...
www.tcp.com/doi/smoon/movie/s.html - 53k - Cached - Similar pages

Live Reviews

... Highly Evolved' is a short-sharp-**shock** of devastating ... around the hall, leaving you in absolute **awe**. ... When considering that The **Reindeer** Section is comprised of ... www.angelfire.com/sk2/mentalmusic/copy_of_Live.html - 98k - Cached - Similar pages

[PDF]EDITOR'S NOTE
File Format: PDF/Adobe Acrobat - View as HTML
... The Idaho Press Tribune's article was a **shock** to me ... signs that ranged from "Honk for Peace" to "Stop Operation Blood for Oil." I chose the Honk for **Peace sign**. ... www.albertson.edu/coyote/0203/Issue62002.pdf - Similar pages

[DOC]The Tale of "Snow Hex and the Seven Sprites", Formally Known as ...
File Format: Microsoft Word 2000 - View as HTML
... is actually a blimp carrying a sleigh with blow-up **reindeer** in front ... AndrAIa watches on in **awe** and blushes slightly ... Dot has a look of **shock** on her face which is ... www.geocities.com/andraias_log/ PrincessDaimonsLover.doc - Similar pages

Fandomination.net | If you build it... They will come...
... his feet touched the ground gently, absorbing the **shock** of impact ... And to top it all off, Santa's **reindeer** seemed to ... The other three stared in silent **awe** as Ami ... www.fandomination.net/?mode=fanfic&FanficID=2521 - 76k - Cached - Similar pages

And this is what I have to work with. My first step is generally to go through and de-bold the bold parts, put everything in the same font size, remove some ellipses and paragraph returns, and delete all the colored header text, unless a particular word or phrase there strikes me as title material. That leaves me with

Rebel Flag Moneyclip Red Panda Earrings Red Panda Pendant Reindeer Pendant Road Bombs Pendant 3rd Army Pendant 7th Cavalry Pendant Shock & Awe Pendant

is actually a blimp carrying a sleigh with blow-up reindeer in front. Luna watches on in awe and blushes slightly ... Usagi has a look of shock on her face which is

Highly Evolved' is a short-sharp-shock of devastating ... around the hall, leaving you in absolute awe. When considering that The Reindeer Section is comprised of

The Idaho Press Tribune's article was a shock to me ... signs that ranged from "Honk for Peace" to "Stop Operation Blood for Oil." I chose the Honk for Peace sign.

is actually a blimp carrying a sleigh with blow-up reindeer in front ... AndrAIa watches on in awe and blushes slightly ... Dot has a look of shock on her face which is

his feet touched the ground gently, absorbing the shock of impact ... And to top it all off, Santa's reindeer seemed to ... The other three stared in silent awe as Ami

From here on, it's mostly a matter of whittling and shuffling. I pare away unwanted words, rearrange blocks of text, and fit it all into a new lineation system (I might choose to retain the formal scheme that has already suggested itself in the existing layout, but not in this case). I never add anything that wasn't already there (except for an occasional punctuation mark or capitalization, etc.). The first run-through at this stage might leave me with:

The Reindeer Section

Rebel Flag Moneyclip Red Panda Earrings
Red Panda Pendant Reindeer Pendant
Road Bombs Pendant 3rd Army Pendant
7th Cavalry Pendant Shock & Awe Pendant

a blimp carrying a sleigh with blow-up reindeer
Luna watches on in awe and blushes slightly
Usagi has a look of shock on her face

a short sharp shock devastating the hall
leaving you in absolute awe

signs that ranged from "Honk for Peace"
to "Stop Operation Blood for Oil"
I chose the Honk for Peace sign

a blimp carrying a sleigh with blow-up reindeer
AndrAIa watches on in awe and blushes slightly
Dot has a look of shock on her face

his feet touched the ground gently
absorbing the shock of impact
Santa's reindeer
stared in silent awe

Beginning to look more like a poem, but...does it *cohere*? My tinkering urges are not yet fully satisfied. Since I started with only six results (my optimum target number is anywhere from 40-70 results), this could easily end up being a pretty short poem by the time I finish scratching away at it. If I do decide to give it another sweep-through, it might end up as this nearly haiku-brief stanza:

Short Sharp Shock

leaving you in a
blimp carrying a sleigh
with blow-up reindeer
rebel flag moneyclip
honk for peace sign
shock & awe pendant
absorbing the impact

Looking back, I worry that I might have lost something with the massive deletions—especially the "refrain" with the changing women's names, which I liked at first and still do a little. At this point, however, the exercise is exhausting itself, and to tell the truth, the poem overall is probably not a "keeper" anyway. The entire process is hit-and-miss, much like standing over a hole in the ice with a fishing pole. Nevertheless, I've found that with the right synthesis of search results and authorial "adjustments," it's a process that can excite my compositional brain in ways that are very useful, and that help me to think about what happens when one composes in the "normal" way as well. The exaggerated Jakobsonian selection-and-combination approach creates the fiction that the poet is working not just with a source text, but with a very small *language*, the *only* language available in the circumstances. This language like all languages is marked by its preoccupations, which have been placed there in part by the poet (who selected the search terms) and in part by the cross-section of the population that exchanges its views, sells its wares, tells its stories, and so on, over the web.

How is all this different from refrigerator-magnet poetry? In many ways, it's not. But because the poet is actively determining at least a portion of the "subject matter," and because the combinatorial decisions invariably reflect back on that initial determination (though they reflect on other things along the way as well), intention enters into the equation in a novel way. Intention is involved in the composition of a magnet-poem too, but there it is simultaneously more and less con-strained. It is more constrained in that all the magnets have been chosen for you in advance—your selection options are essentially limited to the purchase of the kit—and less constrained in that you do not have a motivated set of concepts driving the entire writing operation. These initiating concepts ensure that the poem will be *about* something (e.g. Bush's "shock & awe" bombing campaign), even if only obliquely and absurdly.

Sought poems place the poet at the mercy of the raw material in a way that is different from "normal" composition only in degree; we are always constrained by the limits of our language, and this method simply puts extra emphasis on the constraints. That could be a general definition of poetic form, or of *meter*, and maybe sought poetry is a metrics above all. Because the rules impose sources rather than durations or rhythms, however, the prosodic factor cannot be separated from the thematic. This way of proceeding leaves a good deal of room for individual stylistics, since each poet will have an entirely different set of instincts about how to rearrange the sought material. Looking back at the initial search results, for example, I can imagine wanting to retain the format of the headers and URL info, and perhaps even the color of the text they appear in, making the poem mimetic of its originary context. My impulses direct me toward a more classically columnar lyric strophe, and thus the obsessive re-shaping, which can sometimes result in neo-Imagist severity or worse.

I don't entertain any notion that when I scavenge these voices and viewpoints I am somehow *representing* their speakers. They are unrepresentable once they go through the Google grinder. The useful thing about Google from the poet's perspective is its simultaneous scariness as an instrument of total surveillance (it can and will track you down, no matter where you are) and undiscerning lack of frontiers (it may track down those who are tracking you down in the process). What I seek in such sought poems is not a new type of poetic subjectivity. Rather, I'm looking for instances of articulation (or yes, inarticulacy) in which the poetic object takes on an immediacy that is the product of its embeddedness in a fresh (if not always fresh-smelling) cultural discourse. Though this embedded object is compromised in its ability to deliver anything like an "objective" account of its surroundings, the sought poem not only acknowledges this limitation, but expects and exploits it.

Cal Bedient

THE MOON'S THE WAGON MASTER OF THIS TRAIN, REPEATTED FROM FIFTY BAYONETS, DUN THAT THERE TO CHEAT US OUT OF ITS HAR

My rangers rode to washboard banjos when all nature seemed a graceful group of senoritas sobbing in the shade of orange and pomegranate trees. I could have been a conscience in those days, a little seat: not so wide as to pussy, but I darked and lassoed and dragged the wooden Savior through the plazula, who was hung on a cross hisself like the villagers done me and skinned me besides.

On the night of my burial "it is a hot summer evening" there was 60 of us in the box talking small seethe like fingernails strumming absent-mindedly on the washboard. Jumped out and with a little "Hebe" wore no stockings painted the wild figures of "la Jarabe." The flamenco flounce of starlight catching at the feet of the drummer boy.

Maj. Bliss asked would I make a clean breast of it. Light my ducteen with your har, Major, I said (Reader, *sabe que es pulque*?) and executed a flank movement on the dining room table where the beeves grew in clumps and gained a good if bloody position (though a colored gentleman said "God bless you honey, dis chile kept one of dose places hisself"). Coyotes warwhoooped like greasers from the barran waste no mustang in Mexico could overtake my Kentuck past two rivers kept my course by the stars. But seven of me were found under a tenderloin steak with Ramonda our earless prize and damnably dealt with.

Our dragoons played poker with money they took from the corpses did look at them with green stone eyes came unpleasantly near in the moonlight. My pillow a dead mexican the horses was breathing quiet my slumbers did not refresh me. Next day in Saltillo an Escopette ball passed through the cantles of my saddle and emasculated my John Bulls. I asked the government for $10,000 recompense who had given my all in a country of chaparral justice when life was a crayon stump for painting a naked Senorita on a washboard.

Fifty of me was sentenced to be hanged at the village of San Angel, four was hanged at Mixcoac, and six more sang at the Fortress of Chapultepec like a storm standing on a wagon, its arms and legs mottled and blackened from being tied off, the choir already pricking electrics, abandoned. But we said I will live to eat the goose that will fatten on the grass that grows on yer own grave, Colonel, and on the graves of Quitman, Twiggs, and Worth, and we swung out then and our bodies kicked and rubbed against each other like Florida men, oh we danced then like flushed and florid Florida men

in the days when a great space was a new page and a pimp and a big woman-legged wagon come along and rescued us, so as to outrage the methods, straw-tickle the beetle of the story the usual destiny of the imagination. And a whish-whish of washboard music shone directly on the eaglefeather necks of *los barbarians del norte*. We was large and exhuberant and ripe and truculent as any would wish to look upon on the trail was life then on the sightless trail when our hats was occupied and arisen.

Elisabeth Murawski

AFTER THE FLOWER

> "And where shall we go?
> Ask the submerged things"
> —Pablo Neruda

Neruda molts in his diving suit.
The hose and shoes erode,
the metal sheath waves in slow

motion, lily on a stem.
Called to the supper that lasts,
he has lost all boundaries,

speaks to the dead, to the rose
on pilgrimage, his words like doves
set free from a flood.

It is communion at its most extreme,
the total loss of what was thought
to be essential, a kingdom

of equals at table
destined to become and become.
Submerged things fall apart,

yield to the weight of water,
an emerald city. Neruda hobnobs
with the ribs of a whale,

swims into curves of calcium
spouting song like a troubadour
sworn to lady earth.

Jason Nelson

ABRIDGEMENTS OF SPECIFICATIONS, MARCH 1881

2479. Manufacture of Chairs, Seats & c.

cramping apparatus creates, a leveling or the bottom
of the vertical holes or castors cringes in upholster

2553. Propelling Steam Vessels

There are rods connecting cranks and paddles and applying
them for propelling the three   or twelve
or more than five   three-row cranks.
Each is immersed to receive a curvilinear motion,
drawn in the return strokes of ascend.

2838. Machine for Cutting Keyways or Grooves in Pulleys or Wheels

The   principle   feature improved
cutting slots employed in the ordinary   slotting or planing form.
Direct steel axis, in right angles to length and end and travel
free from milled heads with undetermined changes of motion.

2914. Chemicals for Purifying Vitiated Air

air in tunnels passes
caustic alkali,   lime,   purity,   iodine
forced between its own doubled chemical   swinging
a pack in the last packed swing

2931. Facilitating the Removal of Window Sashes

Its lower half, a metal box, slide inserted in a movable style.
Outer recess is entirely detached, drawn away
in large asking   lines of rope in knotted ropes.

2968. Connecting Warp to the Warp Beam in Looms

A piece of canvas attached by loops or cords or blues and substitutes metal hooks.

2976. Manufacture of Hollow Articles

Paper pulp or paper on a perforated shape   regains oxidized oil   composition and heavy pressure by dies. Reduced in plasticity by boiling's suspense in suitable boils.

2986. Ring Frame Bobbins for Throstle Spinning

Open ends of ring frame bobbins, placed cups in position formed in a frictional connection   and invention's various steadiness, steadies the considerable momentum.

3025.1 Electric Light

A single alternate current   volta meters in series
and electric on one pole   fitting the glass mold.
acidulated water   interpose   any portion or portion's surface

3160. Fountain Pens

The writing end of the instrument,
                                        independent from the clearing.

3175. Apparatus for Calculating

The machine is set at zero.
pins placed in relation   to five plus seven
crane   plate   turned   a fifth gear wheel when
the opposite glazed slot   revolves
seven   numbers further

3227.   Electric Telegraphy

A novel system producing intelligible signals
distanced by making and breaking in transmittance
induced across in current's primary.

3230.   Antiseptic for Preservation of Meat

best proportions   found in one atom of borax
to six atoms of boracic acid   in ten parts by weight
evaporated and the consistency   dissolved
syrup, dried and ground to powder

4910.   Disintegrating Apparatus and Machines

An instantaneous stop designed for the ending
action of machine's least empty parts.

Chris Forhan

DECIDUOUS

I call the maple disconsolate—
the way it turns jaundice-yellow, hurling
its leaves to the ground in a windy fit.

I've watched it through the window all morning
feeling it draw my regard
away from and toward myself.

The maple's score is a dirge for organ and cello.
My score is not as I learned it.

I kissed her. I didn't think I'd do that.

The tree stands in drizzle, stripped and tense
as if it has something to say
and can't say it.

I've loved the sound of saying
it's a cave, a snug nothing, I inhabit—

but she may be traipsing through leaves
this moment on a nearby street
in those blue mud boots, that green coat,
and the maple has taken on a stoic look,
surrounded by all it has given up.

It is the darkest copper. Her hair, her eyes.

I should step outside.
I should let the various parts of me
fall on the lawn
where she'll happen upon them,
bend down, and gather the best of them
into her arms.

Chris Forhan

IN THE VERY TEMPLE OF DELIGHT,
VEIL'D MELANCHOLY

At a hint you were happy, she'd want you
to picture a fistful of dirt
skimming across your coffin lid.

Joy was tragedy waiting to happen—
a candleflame wavering near the kitchen curtains,
a toddler forgotten at the edge of the pool.

When she called you down to the dock to gaze
at the twilit lake, you knew she'd glimpsed
the skeleton rowing his little skiff.

Then when, chilled, almost invisible
to each other in the dark, you turned to walk
back home, and she kissed you hard, she meant it.

Chris Forhan

IT COULDN'T HAVE BEEN HELPED,
IT WAS FOR THE BEST

When the loved one, lost, lives at last
only in memory, no longer in the frenzy
of one's wish that the film rewind on the reel
and breath blow back
and the snake repeal its bite;

When one has mourned, then chosen
to mourn, then been distracted out of mourning;

When one has forgiven oneself the disconsolate songs
that seemed, upon reflection,
a thoughtless flaunting of the self;

And one has almost forgotten
the doomed excursion beneath grief's theatre:
the reckless mission of rescue into the cellarage,
the backward glance that only made the lost love
lost again,

      and one has gone on living
till hardly a cell in the body is left that knows
how one wept
for the stopped heart to stutter and pump again;

When one has come to feel
it is a comfort simply to sit still
within the fading days
and watch the vast shadow of evening reach
the farthest edge of the yard, like a lid slid shut—

Why wouldn't he press his palms against his ears
amid the whispers
about how winter's wail was merely a false alarm,
how spring's big promise is scenting the air with strawberry
and setting sprinklers on the lawn,
how the stone has rolled from the tomb?

Richard P. Gabriel

ESSAY: NERVOUS EYES—AN INTRODUCTION TO THE THEORY OF CENTERS

The second most difficult mystery about poetry is what it is. For three thousand years critics have debated this concern. In the mainstream, we think of poetry as more intense than prose, "[conveying] heightened forms of perception, experience, meaning, and consciousness in heightened language" (Preminger 938), perhaps stranger, more musical. Being musical brings to mind sounds and noise, repetitions, echoes, variations, melody playing off harmony, density. Looking at art we frequently see the same kinds of density and echoes. Poetry has something that sets it apart from prose, and the question has always been whether we can capture that essential unknown.

The main complicating factor is aesthetics—by which I mean a predefined set of principles or guidelines for judging whether a piece is beautiful or acceptable. The real question is whether there is something that underlies the aesthetic question and which would lead us to say, for example, that even though a particular poem is ugly, unattractive, or unacceptable, it is clearly poetry.

I believe there is something underneath our judgment of art, including poetry, that guides our viewing and eventual understanding or appreciation or perception of it as art. The theory of centers essentially asserts that there is a process of perceiving an underlying *poetic order*, which begins before any cognitive assessment and continues through the most detailed of analyses.[1] Poetic order comes from a set of observables called "centers" and their relationship as a field that underlies every poem. The denser the set of centers and the stronger their relationships—according to a taxonomy of relationships that is part of the theory—the more "poetic" or "heightened" is the language of the work.

Centers and their perception are orthogonal to aesthetics and form the necessary fabric of art; and unlike beauty, centers are not contingent, though cognition and hence, culture and taste are needed to make the most detailed map of them. To say it another way, no text can be considered a poem unless it demonstrates a high degree of poetic order.

The definition of a center is complex. Centers exist only within a field, which means that when we try to find them using our cognitive faculties, we need to go through an iterative process in which we first tentatively identify potential centers, and then new possible centers are found and pulled in and others are thrown out. This continues until the field or fields settle down, or the reader simply stops. In normal reading, the field of centers is perceived as poetic order, quality, density, heightened language, or poetry. When we say that some text is a poem, we mean that it has strong poetic order, and when we say that a passage of prose is poetic, we mean the same thing. When we say that we continue to be drawn to a poem over and over, finding new things each time, it could be because the field of centers as perceived is constantly changing as centers are apparently added and removed according the strength of relationships, just as the surface of a pond forms changing patterns of peaks and valleys after a stone or two are thrown in.

To a first approximation, a center is anything that appears within the larger whole as a distinct and noticeable part within a complex of other related parts. Centers appear because they have noticeable distinctness, which makes them separate out from their surroundings and makes them cohere, and it is from the arrangements of these coherent parts that other coherent parts appear.

To be more concrete, a center is any place in a poem that attracts attention. A pair of rhymes attract attention, and each word in a rhyming pair is a center, and the pair of words that rhyme taken together form a larger center. A stress is a center as is an unstressed syllable. So are images, pieces of syntax, lines, the title, the stanzas, sounds, logical connections, and just about any craft technique poets study and use.

A center can be anything the eye falls on and then returns to. Watching what the eye focuses on, and noting how many times it lands on something, we would eventually see the pattern of the most distinct field of centers.

Let's look at an example: "Lourdes," by Bill Knott. This is a good example because, unlike major poems, it is not so full of centers that the concept appears meaningless, nor is it so minor that it is difficult to appreciate the idea of the density of centers adding up to a rich poem:

Lourdes

There are miracles that nobody survives
No one comes screaming of where what when
And these are the only true miracles
Since we never hear tell about them—

Since we never hear tell about them
It increases their chance of being common
Everyday events without witness without
Us even—how absently close we brush

Teeth sneeze cook supper mail postcards
In contrast official miracles take a far
Off locale some backwater—or podunk
Which although unverifiable is visitable

Not pop the map but part the pilgrim's
Lips it springs up hospitals hot dog
Stands pour in testosteroniacs pimple
Victims but most of all cripples—their

Limbs misled and skewed and crisscross
Like—roadsigns that point everywhere
On a signpost bent over a weedy crossroads
In the boondocks of a forgotten place

Some of the initially apparent centers are marked. These represent about half the total number of centers found in this modest poem. Centers are not isolated, but reinforce each other in named patterns. The most prevalent centers in this poem are ones I've termed: Alternating Repetition, Echoes, Contrast, Gradients, and Deep Interlock and Ambiguity. Under the theory, there are also ten other patterns or characteristics of centers—ways that centers connect with each other and create a fabric which is the poem's text. The names of these other patterns are: Strong Centers, Levels of Scale, Boundaries, Positive Space, Good Shape, Local Symmetries, Roughness, The Void, Simplicity and Inner Calm, and Not-Separateness. Not every poem has centers with all 15 of these properties, but it is a rare good poem that is not packed with centers.

Let's look at some of the named patterns of centers.

Repetition is the key for poetry—we expect to see some sort of recurrence, either of sound, image, sense, rhythm, or syntax among other things. Repetition creates a uniform field or cohesive pattern. It echoes our sense of rhythm even when the repetition isn't specifically of rhythm. Not only in poetry but everywhere in the world we see repetition as patterns of visual objects, and even at the atomic level repetition is crucial (for crystalline structure, for example). Repetition is the basis for symmetry. Some connect song and poetry. The shared characteristic is a density of centers with a strong measure of repetition, especially rhythmic repetition. Even though not all music is rhythmically regular, it is still music, and similarly a poem without regular rhythm is still a poem.

Repetition by itself is boring and can become an assault. Most of the repetition we find attractive or compelling is repetition with interspersions, like iambic meter, non-couplet rhyming, or a back beat. What appears between repetitions are tied together and also to the repetitions.

In this poem, the word "miracles" is repeated three times, but not after the third stanza; like many Bill Knott poems, there is heavy sound repetitions and echoes such as "where what when," "without witness without," "teeth sneeze," "unverifiable is visible," "not pop the map but part the pilgrim's/lips it springs up hospitals," and "pimple...cripples"; the last line of the first stanza and the first line of the second are the same; "everyday" and "even" almost line up; the last line of the second stanza starts and ends with words that nearly rhyme. That is, we see repetition of words ("miracles"), sounds (p, wh ess, ee, v, pl,), lines ("since we never..."), and images ("backwater," "springs up," "pours in," and "weedy"). In most cases, the repetition is not immediate but with other centers between.

Echoes are like repetitions, except echoes have more to do with family resemblance than exact replication. What this means is that the centers of the poem seem to go together, are made from the same mind apprehending the same sorts of things. When this fails, a part of a poem will feel stuck on, obscure, random, or pasted in. Loose rhyme is an echo, images that hang together form echoes. Marvin Bell calls it "fishing back," referring to the way a good poem will cast a fishing line back to an earlier part of the poem and catch hold of it, figuratively.

One of the most crucial things to a good poem is for its parts to feel integrated—and of course, this means they indeed do need to be parts of the same thing. This means there has to be a thing—the center that is the poem—and its parts need to be family members.

In this poem, echoes occur in the pair of three-word phrases ("where what when" and "without witness without"), and the physical and sonic similarities of "everyday" and "even," "us" and "brush" at the ends of a line. "Backwater" starts a stream of echoes in "springs up," "pour in," and to an extent, "weedy"; "podunk" seems related sonically and denotationally with "boondocks"; "pimple" and "cripples" sonically echo and are nearly lined up; and "limbs misled" is, on the surface, a nice pair of words related by sound, but later we'll see that they are part of a deeper fabric of centers. "Skewed" is noise-wise like "weedy"; "crisscross" is echoed by "crossroads," but also links to "limbs" and has a deeper connection to "miracles"; and "road-signs" and "signposts" share nominal roots and nearly line up.

Many good poems have strong contrasts in them. A strong enough contrast could be looked at as a contradiction. A poem full of life and good noise will also have moments of deep stillness. One place will be approached closely and another merely hinted at. There will be places of strong rhyme and then loose rhyme. A strong rhythmic pattern will be established and a strongly varied passage will contrast it. Stress/unstress is a basic contrast. Images, words, or phrases that go against the grain are contrasts. Without contrast there is nothing: The pure blue of a small patch of sky seen in isolation (however you might do it) doesn't hold our interest at all—it's just a color sample.

In this poem there are several contrasts: "miracles" and "common /
everyday events," "hospitals" and "hot dog/stands" (also connected
through sound echoes and repetitions), and the explicit contrast of
unseen and official miracles.

Almost no good poem, not even a lyric, stays in one place.
Even if the poem is trying to reveal a lyric moment it will do it by
approaching it, shading it, building on it, taking away from a wrong
characterization. In other words, there will be a gradient which the
reader follows to get to the point where the poet already has been
(or would like to know or experience). Without gradient, there is no
contrast and hence the poem is literally nothing. But more than that,
without gradient, the reader is left to either leap from one place to
another—which does not feel like a natural progression—or is plunked
in one place, stuck observing a bland, neutrally stable landscape.

In this poem there is a contracting image starting with a
"backwater," which then "springs up," and its water "pours in" to
the "podunk" which causes the "weedy crossroads." And in general,
the density of centers increases toward the end of the poem.

Deep interlock means that it is hard to pull centers apart in a well-
made poem. It seems difficult to extract a part of the poem that stands as
well on its own as it does within the poem. Another way of saying this is
that each center derives a lot of its power from surrounding centers.
Similarly, when a poem has deep interlock, you really cannot remove
any part of it without deeply diminishing it. When a poem is "too
big," that means that the centers are weak and some centers are not
contributing enough: Its centers are not (and cannot be) interlocked
deeply enough, and therefore the poem is strengthened by removing them.

On a smaller level, paired stress and unstress form deep inter-
lock, as do enjambed lines. Images that cannot be pulled apart are
deeply interlocked. The fact that a poem is so deeply interlocked
makes it seem more like a whole center, something that somehow
must exist. Prose, on the other hand, is more malleable, and a variety
of revisions, additions, and deletions can be made to it without altering
it very much as a whole. The center that is an entire prose piece seems
less inevitable.

Ambiguity is related because when a center is deeply inter-locked with another, it is difficult to see which center is supporting the other (that is, which is the primary center and which the secondary, which is positive space and which negative). Resolving such an ambiguity or at least considering it is one of the great pleasures of reading poetry. Sometimes an ambiguity can seem like an obscurity, but it is often best to not let such feelings dominate our reaction to a poem. In many cases an obscurity arises from the use of an image rather than from simple imprecision or unclarity.

A simple example is the pair "far/Off" and "everywhere/On," which typical Knott enjambment. In some sense they are an echo pair because of the "/O" commonality, but they also form a contrast because far-off implies distance, rarity, and absence, while every-where-on implies closeness, commonplaceness, and presence. These centers are both interlocked and ambiguous.

One of the most intriguing parts of this poem involves this kind of pattern of centers: "limbs misled." First, this phrase is connected to other centers through the ess sounds, but there is the ambiguity of whether "limbs misled" is to be taken as a visual image of misshapen cripples or of the cognitive image of people being misled by the idea of miracles and perhaps organized religions. This ambiguity ties together the two parts of the poem: the highly visual "Podunk" or "boondocks" pointed to haphazardly by "skewed" and "crisscross" "roadsigns" that point all over and the logical argument about what is a miracle and should we take them seriously.

* * *

The theory of centers is about how a poem is apprehended. We hear the rhymes and see the alignments on the page—the rhythm and its playing off of a metrical system are things we respond to that don't necessarily have anything to do with interpretation, meaning, philosophical stance, belief systems, or context, though those things can be part of how some individuals perceive and understand poems. Plenty of centers can be heard or seen in poems in a language not understood at all. And images and connotations or sly references can figure into a set of centers.

In fact, centers enable an interplay between the spatial and the cognitive. Rhymes, lines, start and end words, and stanzas form a geometry on the page, and the geometry is filled out through time as we read from top to bottom. Moreover, images, implications, facts, other poems, and interpretations are cognitive, outside the poem in some sense, but woven into the mesh of centers. Therefore, centers provide a way to look at a poem from the first glance at it on the page through the deepest intellectual analysis.

The theory of centers has proven useful to some poets for revising their own work. Such poets perform the sort of analysis we started on "Lourdes" on their own work—circling centers and connecting them with lines to show the field of them and how they relate—and when they find parts of their poem with a weak field of centers or see that the flow of the field is in a particular direction or incomplete, they can start revising in that direction. I have tested the theory somewhat by examining sequences of drafts of eventually published poems, starting with the first draft without looking at later ones, doing an analysis, finding weak places (and why they are weak), and then seeing how well the poet appeared to follow the advice the center analysis provided. In all the cases I looked at, there seemed to be significant predictive power to the theory.

* * *

Centers in a poem all lead us toward the center that the poem is. A center is not a theme or a meaning. It isn't even, necessarily, an experience shared with the poet. The poet had a compelling reason to write the poem, to create the center we see, and that center is as alive and human for us as for the poet, but the surface argument, story, theme, meaning, or whatever other intellectual characteristics one might think have something to do with poetry may have little or nothing to do with it. Centers are an abstraction of attention and pointing—and of noticing—and though the richest field of centers comes after all levels of analysis are complete, the early field of centers that appears after the first or second reading perhaps speaks the most accurately about whether the text in front of you is, actually, a poem.

END NOTES

1. The theory of poetic order is based on the work of Christopher Alexander, an architect who has spent his career studying what might be called the nature of underlying spatial order. That a set of characteristics connected with the linguistic and textual realm of poetry on one hand and of the three-dimensional spatial world on the other can be related through the common abstraction of a center and attendant patterns and characteristics implies that there may be something fundamental going on, either at the level of the physical universe or at the cultural or biological levels.

WORKS CITED

Alexander, Christopher. *The Nature of Order: An Essay on the Art of Building and the Nature of the Universe: Book 1: The Phenomenon of Life*. NY: Oxford UP, 2001.

Knott, Bill. "Lourdes." *Becos*. NY: Random House, 1983.

Preminger, Alex, and T.V.F. Brogan, eds. *The New Princeton Encyclopedia of Poetry and Poetics*. Princeton: Princeton UP, 1993.

Daniel Halpern

ANTECEDENT

I meant to have time to think this over,
to make something—
not out of cloth or wood
but from a few notes to say

I refused to reinvent the wheel—
in fact, never turned back.
I'd hoped to make something for you, though,
a plausible thing, something out of nothing.

Daniel Halpern

CREELEY'S HEAVEN

If they've
left they're
leaving no
spoor, no
print, no impression,
not even one
damp layer
against stone to
turn in
a thousand years
permanent in stone

only this
passing as in
seasonal,
buds, a world
in color, of
scent, or
leaves dying
just now on
the branch.

Dorothy Barresi

IF GOD WERE A WISEGUY

Finally we understand
his silence,
his distant ruthlessness,
and kiss his ring.

Protection, bought and sold for the cost of a hallelujah, and heaven

brighter than any white-lit
federal city.

We owe the bookies nothing.
We eat antacid with our *pastae fagioli*
and still get our thumbs broken

though we pray
with proper respect, arrogance
mixed with dirty radiance,

not, for once, to a bag of blue indifferent sky,
but to a brass-knuckled,
wire-tapped tough
capable of making us feel important
for a few lousy moments
before the indictments roll in.

Indictments always roll in.
We take the fall.
That much never changes.

But on the long perp-walk into eternity,

where lewd cigar smoke incense
clears or rises to become
one hymn

knocking us to our knees, then,
this divine,
this wholly uncharacteristic
family loyalty:

an angel in a worsted suit leaning in, hisses,

"The boss says thanks. Says
Don't worry.
He'll take care of your wife and kids."

Chuck Rosenthal

SIMPLICITY TOO SOFT

Are you awake my darling in this horrible room with its dance of walls and ghosts, a map of crucifix, a Virgin Larry, your somber pulse upon my ear, in your chest that listless thumping? At you I wave the flag of simplicity. At you I bare simplicity too soft to understand. Who is that phantom shuffling behind you? What is he doing? A soft shoe? Making it snow webs and dreams. I touch your hair. I touch your hair. I want to find one small place inside me where you have never been.

James Doyle

GOING FROM THE PAINTINGS TO THE DESERT

1

The stone bends over
as if it has become too delicate
for its own weight,
as if it is looking down
for a harpsichord
or some other transparent instrument
to play. It is one of the great
stone flowers
painted over and over
by Georgia
O'Keeffe, the place settings
of polished bone
on desert flatland.

2

Though there is nothing
intangible in this New Mexican
landscape, everything
I reach for
recedes from my fingertips.
Touch has to imagine
me, as if I were
the gallery, and the museum
pieces were constantly
on my right or left,
too far beyond
to doubt
any possibility.

3

I am incidental
to the dry air which holds
the sky and rock
in place. If the air
were ever to shift,
even an inch, the entire desert
would crack
like porcelain into shards
I could rub
between my fingers.
But, though my fingers wore away,
I could never polish the shards
back to the sheen
around me today
when the reflections,
like the water that isn't here,
seem to erode me,
and I begin
to imagine myself the rock
that is no longer here.

Tenaya Darlington

TAXIDERMY LOVE POEMS

> "Some change had come over her body.
> Death had given back part of her beauty…"
> —Dracula

Skinning a deer's ear
I have boiled your hairs at the stove,
lashed bells to your ankles so the dead know
all of you is mine. I have grown dizzy
watching you come into focus—your two milk teeth,
the cornfields of my youth in your hair.
All around us, the early birds are dying,
feathers lining the ditch.
Language gets crowded, every bramble bent.
Still you sing out the parts of your body,
counting off limbs that don't even exist.
Dear hairline, dear fingerlings,
until you number in the hundreds,
I will be braced like lightning against the trees
prepared to clap for your mercy.

Mounted Bird, showing the method of binding down the plumage
Like an accident in song, they remove and clean my body,
Late one July, stringing each feather,
rinsing each muscle, taking the closed wing
to run a pin crosswise through a pedestal.
I call home and force the limb bone through the neck.
There is already a nucleus of excelsior
to fill each opening, jaws singing at the boughs,
though no sound comes out.
In bed, it feels we have lost everything about the night we loved –
The iris-dark of it, the tender coupling—
except that you whisper of returning waterfowl,

which keeps me from lashing out
and otherwise adjusting my legs.

Mounting the skins of fishes
Most of the time our bodies are saying yes,
And in the scope of that yes, there are ten coats of varnish,
Giving our days together the burnished finish of scales overlapping,
Of bone honed smooth against a snagless sky.
What bodies slipped into those bodies,
slumping like a pair of trousers, limp with rain,
marked *exhibit A*, for lack of permanency?
Oh my love, I am so glad you have come back to kiss me.
In spite of October, wild apples have grown around us,
bruised by fate, yet persistent.
I am not in search of a lesson,
but the fierce fruit itself, whose fragrance
is not to be forgotten.
May we haunt a hundred tongues
as long as our mouths are preserved.

Michael C. Blumenthal

CIVIC LEADERS

So much virtue in a single room!
The very walls tremble
with the thought of it.
Just think: the weight
of all that goodness!
And such beautiful denials!
Yet everywhere, even here,
life has its way:
somewhere beneath the table
a living hand
reaches out
in search of a knee.

Michael C. Blumenthal

THE GERMANS

Punctual, decent, historically regal,
Their shoes all arranged, and their closets in order,
The Germans are reading the *Tagesspiegel.*

One has a schnauzer, the other a beagle,
They walk in the *Grünewald,* father and daughter,
So punctual, decent, historically regal.

The pit bulls are banned now, despised and illegal,
Their masters all outraged, accused of a slaughter,
While placidly reading the *Tagesspiegel.*

It still has its wings spread, that old German eagle,
On statues and monuments, where once there were borders,
Lofty and hovering, historically regal.

Not spendthrift or miserly, nor overly frugal,
Yet burdened by history, darkened by murder,
The Germans are reading the *Tagesspiegel.*

Proud of their Schiller, and proud of their Hegel,
Of Rilke proud too, and of Goethe still prouder,
So punctual, decent, historically regal,
And what are they reading? The *Tagesspiegel.*

Cammy Thomas

AUTUMNAL

the instruments don't notice
the cold seeping under his door
at a turn in the road
trees red overhead

the end of purity of the body
to live in layers
of cities built on ruins

then the straightaway home
stone wall pruned shocked pines
the field across the street
its stale pond filled with dogs

Jeanne Marie Beaumont

YOUR SIGN IS DIGGER

I'd packed my bags and stood ready to leave in two directions—
Having just driven down from the coast of my excess.
You used a shady answering service that spoke in relative terms,
"I'm your mother," for example (Freud disliked the phone).
She'll get back to you.

In a dream I smoked the peacepipe with my father.
I must have slept on the worry side of the pillow.
Come to your senses:
Does periwinkle blue mean anything to you?
This restaurant makes exceptional fires or fries.

It's breakfast.
Circumstance for which I'm always first to arrive.
While you're late for the party where you'll be named *a force to reckon with.*
(In the ledger of recollection, red eyes of debt.)

On the subway platform a man held a book in one hand,
A hook where his other hand should be.
I tried not to look.
This wasn't a dream so means—nothing?
Salsa music cascaded down the nearby stairs.
(If you've got time, I'd like to kill some dancing.)

O how does exertion become exhaustion?
The letters, letters, letters.
It's not true that objects can't embarrass you.
Unpack my bag, or the tomb of my mind where I buried—
Don't wake the dead, they're unprotected.
Your sign is Digger. What is it you seek?

Here's where we redeem our jarred-up pennies for thoughts.
A pen for your thoughts (Freud had no typewriter).
In red ink on a periwinkle sheet:
"Dear _____, About that dream…"
Too bad I could never read your homewriting.

Ralph Burns

DEE DEE

On Sundays when late afternoon led me
outside into the Coal Pits looking
for her countenance I'd walk the track
punching rock shell with a stick.
I'd find her somewhere and ask whatever
welled out of me—Are you a boy
or a girl? And she would answer
something I don't now remember.
It wouldn't be clear. So my questions, too,
spun in the air. All I saw was ground,
part sun, part shade, and the stick I dragged
which Dee Dee now drew with in dirt.
Sometimes she'd take one long step
then throw a knife near her foot to see
how close she could come to flesh.
I'd watch and listen for hours and I know
I must've cocked my head like a spaniel
when I heard a weeping sound. That's all
I remember, that and the voices which came
for us, the flashlights bouncing through brush,
and the way my mother and father hugged me
unnaturally and urged me to their car.
I simply remember confusion, the sulphur
smell that so pervaded our town, the parting
of two people, the end of a conversation
for no reason I could know. The immaculate
stars over the orange track. The bolt in the rock
which is probably still there,
the laughter which comes from relief,
but whose,
and what do we do which is wrong?

Roy Jacobstein

THE TASTE OF GUAVA

What is that faint whine
that comes suddenly upon us
every once in a while from within
our inner ear, when we expect it least?
6 AM, you're lying in Little Havana,
logy, yet somehow contemplative,
trying to recall the taste of guava
and whether *Uhuru* is Swahili
for *freedom* or *no sweat*—and there
it is again, like a long-ago friend
making a cameo in your memory.
And though it doesn't rest on silent
haunches, it's about as close
as noise can come to silence,
and it departs as swiftly and silently
as any cat, leaving you more mystified
about everything, like why
Grandma always makes beef stew
on Veteran's Day and why she persists
in garnishing her dishes with parsley
when it's so bitter—though it is,
come to think about it, quite a lovely
shade of deep, deep, green.

Ann Humphreys

LESSON IN ADULTHOOD

Waking up to adult life, stone in the jaw.
You'll never be mirrored by your father

again...what of it? Now is the time
to drive to work, to snap on the news

or let some other adult's teeth
grind into your neck—let's get over this

as grownups. Pop a beer, measure up
some gin and vermouth, make it sloppy.

Perc up a pot of coffee, extend a cigarette,
let a hand dangle out a car window

but don't let your kids do it.
Get a cardiogram.

Breast self-exam, pelvic, regular
dental, hair and nails. Keeping up

with the decaying human form
takes a lot of experts.

Get one to teach you how to come, for fuck's sake,
before your bunged-up female equipment

dies childless, you know? If you can't manage
to create a life to nurture, you could at least get

over yourself enough to offer some guy
the sight of you conquered, helpless.

Carrie Bennett

LATE AT THE HOUR

of course we anticipate this
the light falling through the screen that way

how does something look
                      like gold
in the back of my throat a house of numbered rooms

we were the couple
swimming in the gulf
                the only two
the sky the water
the pin trees twisting
the sand

                   when all the days
started leading away
              then

Carrie Bennett

COVERED THE MARK

the hand no longer rests
                    what flies flies away and
there is three
of everything

where do the lined figures go
                              the bird's wings
fall off
              a formal breath
in the wrong element

the depths of which are gone immobile are stationary horizons
this is the sum of a bent figure

                    a hole in the ground
fills
              metal and water under each :
                                        it opened the night
                                        opened   the   eye   stitched
shut

the lines eventually end the day with too much

Joan Aleshire

FREEDOM OF SPEECH

When we were free of her,
and old enough to laugh,
we repeated the incident
none of us had seen, but none
disputed—that Mrs. B. flew into a rage
fiercer, one day, than her habit,
over some child's failure or mistake,
and stamped her small foot,
shod in those pointy-toed high-heeled pumps
she favored, stamped like Rumpelstiltskin
until her ankle broke under the weight
of her impotence. One of those women
who has no choice but teaching
grade school or believes the small
can be controlled, in our small world,
she was everywhere—tutor, overseer,
director, commander, coach—
with no classroom of her own,
able to swoop—Tennyson's eagle
like a thunderbolt—on our flaws:
her eyes, red nails, nose, sharp toes,
hair permanently controlled,
everything we could see about her
honed to an unforgiving edge.

As if we were all in training for the C.I.A.,
she oversaw the maps we made
of ancient empires, tracing the borders
onto thin paper that allowed
only the heavy outlines to show through.
Quick to spot a smudge or wavering line,
she bent over our work, perched

on our desks for closer inspection
of unpromising executions—mine,
where revisions left tell-tale blots and erasures.

Her scorn even then seemed absurd
to me: maps weighed lightly
against the high grades and gold seals
the regular teachers put on my work.
I had no fear when I found her
the coach of our 6th grade graduation,
where I was chosen to recite.
At 11, self-important, self-confident,
I loved to take the stage,
and said from memory in my usual style
the rhymes I'd been assigned.

Silly, simple to remember, easy
to say—a *jingle*—I thought
I'd done it perfectly at rehearsal,
and was amazed to hear Mrs. B.
command, *Do it again*—but differently,
stressing the syllables she
would stress, changing my cadence,
repeating the stupid words,
which she had probably written,
until I could make no sense of how
I *should* sound, and stepped up
on the flower-filled stage at graduation
queasy and trembling, for the first time
terrified to speak.

I said the verses as if my mouth
had forgotten to move, sure only
I'd remembered and uttered them
aloud, believing my voice, my way
of speaking, unalterably wrong:

the beats and pauses that made
my own music mistaken,
so that for years I shrank
from speaking to groups of more
than three, let alone a crowd,
innocence of a plump, prominent child
gone—until the night in high school,
chosen to lead vespers, expecting
the usual chasm to open as I stepped
the miles from my seat to the makeshift altar
in the oak-paneled gym, but found
the words I had to say—common prayers,
my own adolescent attempts to be wise—
coming through my mouth, as if I
were only the means to the utterance,
and my body, my own voice with its
particular sound and cadence,
had dissolved into the candlelight,
into the broad river of speech
I at that moment so wholly believed,
I trembled not from fear, but words' force.

Mark Halperin

ON CERTAINTY

Think of the sick man, the accident victim
at that moment when he knows
clearly there is no saving him—
his as the certainty you crave. Suppose,

unwittingly, we just go on mixing hope
with understanding, until the horizon
shrinks to a point, or a single note
blots the rest out, and we've nothing to pick from.

Doesn't it fit the endings we intuit—
of innocence, of love—their calm
extent, the almost infinite
flatness they leave us going on and on?

Maybe certainty is growing old
all at once, finding you stand on ice
thick enough to support you. The cold
creaks beneath, or maybe it's only lies.

Mark Halperin

PARAKEET

Mornings, she'd hop my shoulder for a ride,
take off for the blinds, or like a lover, nibble
my earlobe with such persistence I had to
brush her off—and struggled through illness,
as though called back. When I saw her

on her side and righted her, she let me
stroke her flank and head with my finger,
keeping herself upright, vertical, just tipping
forward, stretching her neck out, black eyes
undimmed, without sound or stir, as she died.

Her absence hovers like a swelling drop,
the words she almost knew in two languages.
She'd nudge a pencil to the table edge,
watch it stall, then lower her beak and push
again, waiting, as it toppled, for the crash.

James Cervantes

A VILLANELLE RETURNS FROM WAR

You have to make sense now.
Planes are in the air.
You have to speak up

before planes. You've bought all
there will be to buy. Say something
plain, make bye-bye. Tell everyone

you need this and this. What?
No flower in the kit?
In the kitchen, panes warm up,

whistle. See why there is no steam:
It's all fire and sand. It's pain
less flour, salt, and petals. Yell,

whistle, say some lower the living,
raise the dead, craft the air. Oh, and
bring people, take people. Ports

are drawers of the sea,
tables of land. Sit down, be sensible,
say something before you take off again.

James Cervantes

AGAINST CLEAN LINES

"I once believed a single line in a Chinese poem could change forever
How blossoms fell..."
—Gary Sullivan

Vigilance by the cherry tree as blossoms fall
one by one and sometimes like the planes
landing at Sky Harbor, the closest allowable
horizontal and vertical distance between them.

Once, on a gusty day, they fell in quatrains,
as unbelievable as dandelion seed's cosmic pendulum.

And on a windless day, one fell straight down
as if along a plumb line. Our words, our pun.

In the desert there are updrafts.
Thus a lazy spiral, an ever-so-brief stop, then ascension,
imparting to a blossom the floating gut
of an elevator stop.

Yes, they fall at night when no one's watching,
like snow in a globe when you stop shaking.

Add moonlight and steady wind and there are the Leonids.

Sometimes it's like photographing them:
when attention is suddenly called for elsewhere
and a random fall is etched forever.

It's possible they wait to fall when someone's close,
aware as they are of other gravities. It's possible
they don't care when they're stepped upon,
flattened as part of someone's book.

D.W. Cunningham

FROM, BETWEEN

Say distance
were a curiosity…

A finch and feeder
 nearby…suspended…

A millimeter gap
between my apposed finger
and finger.

We've pulled up season-wise,
the pint and I,
outside.

The finch pecks;
I trim a lexicon: out

Go "hobby" and "cult";
staying are "stem," "gothic,"
"Euclid"
out…"sect"…in…"set."

It's a quick routine
appearing slow,
like one's hand reaching
for the glass
or the hops-head
in decline

Or (beloved recall)
 bundles
of *The Racing Form*

under my father's bed
  going to dust,

His margin-glosses
  ending up here

In the light and sky
and water on wood.

James Brock

WIND ACROSS THE EVERGLADES (1958)

I. After the First Dailies—Budd Schulberg Is Pleased by Burl Ives

Burl Ives, yes, God love that fat, pink
s.o.b., God love him for loving
Hemingway and cracker rot gut, love him
for getting on my ass about Elia Kazan
and HUAC, even when I tell him Jesus
Henry Christ, give it a rest, that's ancient
history, and besides, I tell Burl, I saved
Kazan's soul from that limp-wristed *Streetcar*
romantic hoo-hah, penned *Waterfront*
after Mailer dared me to write a real movie,
which got me the Oscar, a wad of money,
and a way for me and Stuart to do
our own movie, a real Technicolor Florida western,
with sex, strippers, rum, guns, and
bigamists, and I show Burl the real liberal
deal, those gray subplots: 1) the Jewish
shopkeeper and his daughter staking their place
on the frontier, 2) a real Seminole Indian love tragedy,
and 3) the whole conservationist sweep of
the story. Big-hearted Burl, the simp, bear
hugs me. He says he loves me, after I let
him improvise with the rubber moccasin
snake, laughing at what Freud would've made
of it, but happy, he told me, to be playing
the outlaw Cottonmouth, nobody's fool,
and happy that I made the real louses
the Lillie Langtry's and societal belles of London
and New York and their dandified love
of hats and egret feathers and their stupid
husbands, happy, that big-hearted happy soul

God surely has blessed. We trade
shots with the cast, and green Chris
Plummer, who plays the game
warden, is the first to go, until it's just
me and Burl and that sweet fiddling Totch Brown,
who tells us both we'd do fine in
the 'glades. Burl laughs and says, hell, Totch,
we're already here and we're in it for keeps.

II. Budd Schulberg Casts Emmett Kelly

Here's the joke: cast Emmett Kelly, after
Jimmy Stewart stole his role from DeMille,
let him be Bigamy Bob (a sideshow name),
sport a real week's growth beard, besotted
clothes, even a dead felt hat, and the joke,
to give him lines to speak. Kelly talks! And
boy, how he talks, of leaving six wives and
six lawyers behind at the border of the Everglades.
The art of it, too: I write on the script—*no*
goddamn ab libbing, no goddamn
jokes! Kelly plays it straight, as he said he
would when I found him wintering in
Sarasota, as I was trolling among the Ringling
misfits, and there was Emmett Kelly
mixing vodka and orange juice, telling
everyone how this was the right way to enjoy
Florida. He was suspicious at first, unimpressed
with Nick Ray as the director, even with
Gypsy Rose Lee coming out of retirement
to sign on, but he got hooked when I
told him that Tony Galento was going to be in
Burl's gang along with Bigamy Bob. "You know,
Budd," he says, "you're a better boxing writer
than movie writer," and by God, if he isn't

right. Emmett himself saw the genius
in the role, saw how his own life slipped,
not Chaplinesque at all, not even like Keaton,
but a quick slip off the edge of the world.

III. *Johnny Guitar*

So Ben Gazarra jumps ship as the lead
at the last minute, and here's the classic
Hollywood moment, and I am leaving it
to Nick's gut instinct to cast the right man
as our lawman and who has the romance
of the outlaw in his heart, the right man
big enough to face down Burl Ives, the right
man big enough to be humbled
by the 'glades and learn a thing or two
from the crackers in Chokoloskee. I trust
Nick, and I am thinking *Rebel* and
James Dean, or better, I am thinking *Johnny Guitar*
and Joan Crawford, as hard dressed as any
man, a good and clean shot, a face
you wouldn't cross. Nick says, "Christopher
Plummer." I don't know the guy, and
when he comes off the plane in Miami, I
see the opening scene in the movie, someone
weak and vain, the outsider lawman
coming into town, a little effete, but not too much
in a Sal Mineo way. But in the end, will Plummer do,
someone who's strong enough
for Cottonmouth's poison, strong enough
to break Joan Crawford's neck?

IV. Budd Schulberg at Ted Smallwood's Store

Although Ted's daughter, all southern gritted
and kind, warms to me, or rather, to a man
who doesn't seem all Hollywood and money,
who rightly admires Eisenhower, who hasn't
lost his way, I am looking for the clue here in
this store, where the settlers here killed
Ed Watson, a murderer himself, in 1910. She
says, "I don't remember it at all, but Father,
rest his soul, did not partake in the event."
Years later, Peter Mathiessen asks me
about the movie, my take on Guy Bradley's
death, and tells me he's stitching together
a trilogy of his own on Ed Watson.
Good luck, I tell him. Stuart and I
lost our shirts. Before
production ended, I published the screenplay
for a few extra thousand dollars, to create
a little pre-publicity, to affirm the film,
a strong man's work. It tanked, too. But before
all that muddle, I was standing in Smallwood's store,
smelling the rot of animal carcasses
drying, thinking of the too close
holocaust, and here I stood,
also in the vibrations of another past. Some
men took aim. Everyone fired. A man fell,
dead, before hitting dirt. The star, I knew,
could never be a man, not even Cottonmouth,
but the Everglades, this smell, this color
and its wind.

Tony Hoagland

ARGENTINA

What I notice today is the aroma of my chiropractor's breath
as he moves in over my supineness, asking me where I bought those shoes
at the same instant that he
                wrenches my head abruptly sidewise
to crack my neck with a noise like popping bubblewrap

It's January, no, it's February, it's Pittsburgh
and I've been so twisted by craving and loneliness and rage,
I feel like curling up on the floor of my room and crying,
"You never loved me anyway, not ever!,"
though I'm not sure who I would be talking to.

Kath says February is always like eating a raw egg;
Peter says it's like wearing a bandage on your head
Mary says it's like a pack of wild dogs who have gotten into medical waste,
     and smiles because she clearly is the winner,

& in Argentina, after the elections,
we hear the old president won't leave office—
literally, they say—they can't get him out of the office!
He's in there with his little private army, eating caviar,
squandering state money on call girls and porno movies—
and if you've done any therapy at all, I think you'll see the analogy.

How did I come to believe in a government called Tony Hoagland?
With an economy based on flattery and self-protection?
and a sewage system of selective forgetting?
and an extensive history of broken promises?

What did I get in exchange for my little bargain? What did I lose?
Where are my natural resources, my principal imports,
and why is my landscape so full of stony ridges?

Having said that much,
having paid a stranger to touch and straighten me,
I walk out the door to my old car in the parking lot
—which, after the slight adjustment of a spring shower,
looks almost new again.

Tony Hoagland

POEM IN WHICH I MAKE THE MISTAKE
OF COMPARING BILLIE HOLLIDAY
TO A COSMIC WASHER WOMAN

We were driving back from the record store at the mall
when Terrence told me that Billie Holliday
was not a symbol for the black soul.

He said, the night is not African-American either, for your

    information,
it is just goddamn dark,
and in the background

she was singing a song I never heard before,
moving her voice like water moving
along the shore of a lake,
reaching gently into the crevices, touching the pebbles and sand.

Once through the dirty window of a train
on the outskirts of Hoboken, New Jersey
I swear I saw a sonnet written high up on a concrete wall,

rhymed quatrains rising from the
dyslexic alphabet of gang signs and obscenities,

& Terrence says he saw a fresco once
of brown and white angels flying
on a boarded-up building in Chinatown

& everybody knows
there's a teenage genius somewhere out there,
a firebrand out of Ghana by way of Alabama
this very minute in a warehouse loft,
rewriting Moby Dick—The Story of the Great Black Whale.

When he bursts out of the womb
                              of his
American youth
with his dictionary and his hiphop shovel,

when he takes his place on stage,
dripping the amniotic fluid of history,
he won't be any color we ever saw before,

and I know he's right, Terrence is right, it's so obvious.

But here in the past of that future ,
Billie Holliday is still singing
                              a song so dark and slow
it seems bigger than her, it sounds very heavy

like a terrible stain soaked into the sheets,
so deep that nothing will ever get it out,
but she keeps trying,
she keeps pushing the dark syllables under the water
then pulling them up to see if they are clean
but they never are
and it makes her sad
and we are too

and it's dark around the car and inside also is very dark.
Terrence and I can barely see each other
in the dashboard glow.
I can only imagine him right now
pointing at the radio
as if to say, Shut up and listen.

Gail Wronsky

REVIEW:
SOMETHING BLACK IN THE GREEN PART OF YOUR EYE by KEVIN CANTWELL
New Issues, 2002. $14.00

"You may be amused at the comparison, but in finishing it I found the same after-taste remaining as after finishing *Madame Bovary*, such a flavor of persistent euphony." Although William James is speaking to Bergson about Bergson's *L'Evolution Créatrice*, the statement seems an appropriate starting point for a review of Kevin Cantwell's deliciously nuanced and copiously beautiful book of poems. In these poems, as the collection's title indicates, "the green part of your eye"—the luxurious, verdant, exotic, and ultimately human world—serves as a frame for the poet's investigation of "something black"—death, of course, but not, as Cantwell warns us, the "familiar darkness" ("Border States," 28).

Here is a poetry informed by lyric intellect, dazzling in its erudition, and yet somehow served up Macon, Georgia style—on a Harley, with a side of dead guitar players and crystal meth. Lush and layered, literate and musical, as if W.B. Yeats had been brought up on Delta Blues— which is not to say that these are by any means easy poems to read. They are drenched with mournful sounds, with dark subjects, with an intimate knowledge of loss. The consolations they offer are in some ways the familiar consolations of poetry: beauty, precision, the exquisite pleasure of experiencing, as in reading Flaubert, something masterfully made. And yet there is a defining, lingering strangeness in this work as well which refuses to console.

The title poem, "There's something black in the green part of your eye," a line from the movie *Chinatown*, begins with a boy wanting to rent a shotgun "just to shoot down mistletoe// from the levee sugarberries," then shows us "a wedding tent's white canvas cloud, through which, like swifts,/tuxed and tailed, black figures disappeared," then shows us a girl in Montreal giving another girl a "shotgun" (19) of illicit smoke—the three images demonstrating movement, relationship, a range of milieu, memory and observation with something just a little bit amiss. Finally the speaker remembers an old friend: "no one I loved or kissed//enough to think I loved, but someone I drove to the river with,/summer gone & the grass deep in her lungs thick smoke in a stream..." (20). He remembers another gun, and a kiss, and the girl's sister, a time when they were "all lit," ending the poem with a "muffled report from inside the house;//that door one of these heart pine slabs that come unhinged,/made that way so a body could go cold & then be carried out" (21). This is a moment of stunning resonance. One realizes that the poem has, of course, led artfully to its revelation (we die) and yet we are nonetheless taken unawares by its finality, by the absence of familiar consolation. It is the moment before *denouement*, the moment before Hamlet offers his conciliatory "Let be." Kevin Cantwell is a romantic poet (like the rest of us—one of "those heart pine slabs that come unhinged") but not remotely sentimental ("made that way so a body could go cold & then be carried out").

Along with loss, ecstasy is summoned in many of the poems here. There is the "narcotic dusk of barn swallows and summer's calendar" (54) in the poem "Dora;" there is a "girl's pale dress// (turning) white to lavender to pink to purple until color itself/hesitates" (48) in the poem "Color and Chance in the Experimental Garden." Even "the rotten smell of the pulp mills" (25) in "End of Summer, Below the Fall-line, Central Georgia" seems enticing and sensuous in the world of these poems.

The poem which most powerfully engages both loss and ecstasy, it seems to me, is "Dido's First Theory of the Lyric," perhaps the finest poem in the book. It begins with "a clerk, reporting//only what had come down to him by whisper; that on a found island—/a fetish sect: women who believed that all must go back//to where they lost their minds with grief; there begin anew" (62). This is of course the task of the lyric poet: to go to the source of pain, of loss, of grief, and write. It's interesting that it is a "clerk" here, telling "only what had come down to him by whisper." Is this the poet modestly and cleverly refusing to reveal himself too fully, too early on in the piece? Is it that a poet is a kind of clerk, ultimately, tabulating debits and credits in compact configurations down a page?

By the end of the poem, Kevin Cantwell has revealed himself, his depth and brilliance, more than fully. By the end of the poem he has also rewritten, replaced, the canonical encounter between clerk and typist in Eliot's *The Waste Land*, that sad and totally unsatisfying bit of Modernist sex ("Well now that's done: and I'm glad it's over") with a love affair, rather much more that a sexual encounter, of breathtaking, go-for-broke lyricism and authority. It contains almost unbearable ecstasy alongside almost unbearable pain. It is formally ingenious, syntactically insistent, and profound evidence of a major new presence in American letters. Allow me to quote the last portion of the poem in its entirety:

> ... & then months later, the stranger arrives at the docks;
> his skin, not touching yet; hers, the desire; his, the touch; rain,
>
> the rain beating leaves to shreds outside their hidden cave; he,
> summoned too soon by the goddess's whisper; she, let down, over her
>
> combs, over her anointing oils; & hers, the pause beyond that
> emptying; her chilled skin flushed before the blood's drain; her hair
>
> rent & her flesh mooned up beneath her fingernails & all the wind-
> shorn candles blown out by a drape ripped open; she, a droop wet
>
> with night on the patio; the date palm's patois rustling: the luff
> of the clerk's murmur; hers, the sea; the sea, before her; she
>
> asking that madness cease; she, saying, if you go do not speak; she,
> from sleep: let me help you with the fire; here is my body, my voice,
>
> the oil; here is my body, my body, the wick; if you go why won't you
> speak? That thirst; that surf; hers, the voice ripped out of the sea;
>
> hers, the servant girl pouring water into a plum-black bowl, the girl
> not knowing what to do; she, the Queen; hers, the porcelain sky
>
> & the boiling pour splitting the ceramic, rim to basin; the painted
> gull split from the painted cloud; the cracking tear: the lightning
>
> lit-up sea.

(62-3)

Alice Templeton

ONE

"One, one, one would be the monotonous response forever."
—George Santayana

Eden, Vermont

Just past Eden I roll the window all the way down
as if a loose-fitting ease I have lost might blow in
with the wind. Late August plays its tricks
on my arm, heat of afternoon sun, chill of air,
what has been and what's to come pressed
into what is. Today I drive, resisting the hours
the church bell tolls—*one   two   three* o'clock—resisting
the instinct to make the usual, thick sense of now.

I wanted to start new, to leave the logical bells behind
and simply live, a being, soft and unbreakable, beside you.
I wanted to start from here, no hindsight, no plot
compelling me. But thought counts, cannot help but count,
fashioning stories, backward, forward, pretending to explain.
Every telling stings: grief is long, my nightwatch, monotonous.

Do I live my life or carry its books? Can I pop a knuckle
and not wish it for the other nine, or spit to the ditch
without comparing how close? *One one one*
has no hands or deeds: the road is, August is, we are
brilliant slips of the sequential tongue, confounding our biographies.
But sparks find mirrors in the dark; hope requires a memory
and we are long past Eden, gulping at wind that can neither cleanse
nor restore us. Back in the town school boys turn pages and pray
for three o'clock—and who am I to resist? Still, time after time,
for the love of beginning, I want the world without me, a watch
without its hands already full; in the cloudswell of every dawn
I want illumination without my shadow cut from its light.

William Heyen

CACTUS

Variance is the square root of the standard deviation
on these evaluation forms, his Chair told Crazy Horse
without being asked. The meeting got worse
like unto such. The Indian decided to become

something tall, green, welcoming to small birds
who could nest in him, & tending, after spring rain,
to flower & seed. The flummoxed Ph.D. wondered
how he could co-exist with all these spines

crowding him. How calibrate a margin of error
for this response? Was that protuberance
from the young buck's forehead about to bloom
pink? He removed his glasses, rubbed his eyes,...

& let's give him this: he knew he had gotten older
in heart than sin. Who was he now? A machine
could graph these forms till Hades froze over,
for all he suddenly cared. He closed his briefcase

for home. Behind him, Formica & linoleum
sprouted foliage, fledglings flew out from holes
into which we peer to where *Tasunke Witko*
continues in his dreams to needle time.

Gaylord Brewer

AMERICA AT WAR

I pass the morning outside
in short sleeves,
forearms bare under March sun.
As I seal the grain
with rags and fruitwood stain,
I wear protective gloves
to keep my hands pristine.
If the plan holds,
this small table will balance
books, and drinks, for many years
in the room where I
control the world,
in the place reserved
beside my old chair,
its threadbare gold
concealed just today, in fact,
beneath a cotton blanket—
all virgin forest, snow-blue peaks,
grizzly as broad as the sky.

David Wagoner

IN PRAISE OF THE HIGH VISCOSITY
OF THE ENGLISH LANGUAGE

Your sluggishness seems well worth
      Muddling in without
            A good excuse. A line
Slogging its short passage
      Through your quagmire
            Without losing both boots
And waddling off off
      Balance will find a better poem
            Than this one now and be
Slipperier at it. Oh, what
      Messes we've all made
            With all our slewfoot efforts
To clarify your nature and how
      Hard you've made it for us even
            To do this little. For sheer
Thickness, no pond bed
      Unsettled by cows wading
            Could ever match what some
Of us poor souls have gone on
      And on stirring up in you,
            Yet we'd have made and said
And done nothing by now
      And would have gone nowhere far
            Faster without you.

David Wagoner

FOR A BALLPOINT PEN

The pen scrawling these lines
Has spent two rainy days
In the gutter, up against bars
Of a storm sewer,
Has been rescued, cleansed,
And redeemed, has been
Through it, in it,
And under it, has survived,
And now wants to roll on
And make its mark, to feel
Once more the beckoning
Of capillary attraction
Down to the final light
Millimeter of darkness,
To have its say,
Whatever still may fall
Under the jurisdiction
Of thumb and index finger
And the callused oval
At the root of the last knuckle
Of the middle finger
Of its maladroit longhanded
Employer who now,
With digital mock-assurance,
Guides it on emptiness.

Dick Allen

LACK OF AMBITION

Gradually, from one side of the sun to the other,
Earth carries my house.

Why write letters
when you can think good thoughts? I send you my good thoughts.

There's a piece of banana-carrot cake in the refrigerator.
Proust lies helpless on the floor, alas!

Yesterday, I opened an empty kitchen drawer
and filled it with nothing but lace and rose petals.

I put a flame to a blue candle
and watched it burn down into the bluest nub.

The housecats laze in and out of my humiliations.
Little stops them from sleeping.

Fame is as fame does.
If I must walk to somewhere, let it be only to a jar of grape jelly.

Work is imagination. No, work is imitation.
No, work is a mine field.

My study's a thousand miles away from my living room.
Upstairs is an infinity.

I like thinking about Kansas because it's so much like a tepid creek.
No one does anything in Kansas but hang out clothes.

I should get up and throw stones into Frog Pond.
I should buy something, anything, a box of cornflakes.

This poem's too heavy to read. It's all weighted down
with George Crabbe. Icicles hang from its roof.

Why do I remember, now,
that old high school song, *Hernando's Hideaway?*

I pulled on one sock and left one sock off
until the tires came home.

Studying nothing's hard. What you want to do
is dream your way into the essence of a tomato.

The computer's been stupid for weeks. Ant-one and ant-zero
lie frozen in spare parts.

Let the wind rake my lawn. Let the sun paint my house forsythia.
I'll wait for a sideways rain to wash the windows clean.

Why not let yourself drown in a pool of relatives,
like most people do?

The theology spokesman said, wearing a long straight face,
We're only here to entertain each other.

It's all temporary.
The road to Maine is better, and Arundel antique shops.

If I got there, anyway,
I'd only fall down.

Dick Allen

LUCK, BE A LADY

Or, if not, be a woman with glasses
walking down a garden path in moonlight,
a gem-encrusted handbag swinging from your arm.
Be a red bandana, a new Circuit City,
the right page at last. When you approach me,
out of the dreck of wherever you've been all my life,
expect my hunger. I've been feeding it old sports sections
and teachers' promises, but now I need to see you in the flesh,
taking your glasses off, removing your makeup,
kicking your shoes towards the door. Luck,
be a reminder of my '57 Bel Air Chevrolet,
carrying me over the tornado roads of upper Ohio,
the Seekers singing, "A World of Our Own."
If, at last, you've decided to meet me,
let there be bananas and milk and cornflakes,
marbles in a dirt circle,
everything gone to whim and the better for it,
for I believe, as Ben Shahn did, that all humanity
lives for Art and lives by Art,
understand it or not. Luck, you chemistry student,
you wild Irish rose, you sit-with-your-back-to-the-wall,
snowstorm just before dawn, astonishing website,
touch my hands with the smallest of your fingers,
lead me to pinecones in the ruins of Detroit,
and when you're done,
disappear slowly, like blank squares in crossword puzzles,
names of those we waited on in old hotels by the river,
someday, somewhere, you and I, dear Luck.

Richard Jones

THE SACRIFICE

Soren Kierkegaard says to suffer
more precisely. Let the bitter soul be
loved by God.

Does he know what he's asking?
When a man has lived even a few years
the heart's a grave, a poor burial plot. Look—

there they lie buried in forgetfulness:
promises, intentions, resolutions,
not to mention the shadows of crimes and lies.

Still, Kierkegaard insists on surrender:
empty the self in tranquil abandon.

He uses words like *unchangeableness*
or *fear and trembling*. He quotes scripture—
purity of heart is to will one thing.

Kierkegaard sounds like God, who asks,
"Have you now anything to complain of?
Though I embittered your childhood and youth,
do you not now have my infinite love?"

For by such bitterness all
are trained to endure, to be love's sacrifice.
Sacrifice, Kierkegaard would insist.
Proof infinite grace has been shown.

Jordan Davis

THE LOOKING

A cerebration, and the Kodiak
Try out, what do we have when we have a clue?
By way of time, I mean. Enough
Data sufficiency problems, and their med/moy
USA, all the captains of industry
Quote Bullwinkle, early and often,
And just as (praise God) you don't price wheelchairs
Just so there is a grapefruit at the heart,
Thrown at my heart by thought
By a hyper proxy. Come back, substitute teacher,
Show me more movies from the fifties,
Those delays and invasions are all I have
Stretching out in the attache,
Looking out across the fog from the dry ice
To decide what goes where on this lacquered stage.

Jordan Davis

POEM

When the song's called "song"
The executives all reading
How to put trash in its place
Will you come be emotionally
Available with me as the ink
Dries will you watch me with tears
In your mouth as I sing along—
Pour you a glass of milk, hey!
A year and some since you couldn't
Go outside and a year since the shades
Came down, let me pour you a glass
Let me pour you a glass of milk, hey!

Jordan Davis

EACH I CHING GOES FISH

Think, act. Think think, act.
Think think think, act. Act.
What's the difference? What's
Difference? One of these kids
Thinks a lot like his mother.

The fish
Go towards
And away

People leaning towards them.

Do I want out?
The shot clock stops.
Los Angeles unrolls its shower mat,
Applies understanding topically.

Will the better light fell me?
Phrase it as a meditation
Yellow sweater
A million meanings gather.

Hear it as imperatives
You will bake a white bread
(The cook book
A species of astrology).

What is decided
Is a bureaucratic mind

No Down
No Monthly
No Parabolic Dish

Tracking the winey keemun
As it circumnavigates my tone.

What is decided
Is marked to market

Bid and ask sleep-deprived
Neoteny out on
An unscheduled sleep holiday

To the baby core of love looks
The moon is melting
On the tree.

Anselm Berrigan

DO SERVICE CHANGES PUZZLE YOU?

perhaps morals and their systems were mutations
to begin with chum, in a bucket, seducing sharks
for one of a billion photo-ops teeth flashing
sustained analysis being a degradation of why we fight
o lord, the train to your pantry needs black gold
ogling the gesture of defiance, sometimes it takes
decades of brutality you've financed to see a dirty dog
drunk, coming at me, second time that I got home
drunk as I could be, there's another mule in the stable
where my mule oughta be, let me tell you about
the way he's not there

Anselm Berrigan

HUDDLE PRESENCE

sizing up a head to fell   I've been talking more to myself

among the eight million lately   catch me mumbling on 7th st.

keep it going   let 'em all in   see cigarettes flower

into public funds   dropping back and letting fly

a long bomb   what I get from the bar is skill

Shakespeare   heroes push buttons

thick fingers   seceding from hands

with renewed faith   in the hitch

hinge   hickey   I've got great huddle presence

Patricia Spears Jones

SHIMMER

how fire begins is easily explained
that's why people hate science

who wants to know
the precise chemical composition of depression?
can't there be mysterious forces
and the loss of shimmer?

when stars explode on summer evenings
must we match their bright fury
with the precise velocity of light?

Radio waves are a wonder to behold—
speech pulsing like sex with a new lover
and can't that be enough?

Joe Amato

BE RIGHT WITH YOU.

First, let us investigate one another
because because because because/ because, just
because. Later, pinned down
at the bar
and pressed to cough up
what could possibly be
meant, we would garble words defiantly
our speechifying to be captured live
by a planetful of red, white & blue

mikes. Ah, well—the markets tank anyway, or
don't, and everyone retires
broke, having proved all
but inadequate. Of course
some of us are made to feel
by others programmed to make us feel
more inadequate than
others. Some of us still
call this *bad vibes*. But let's not argue, OK?
Because because because because/ because
this is the world we so wanted, right?
Knee-high by July, bathed
in sepia, flagging, not to say
weaponized? Just be sure
to pass that bottle of Brunello
before they repossess our thumbs.

CONCLUSION: French squirrels, while squirrels
          are nonetheless less outgoing
          and somewhat more diplomatic
          than US squirrels
          because they're, you know
          French. Beats the shit out of me
          too, but this might suggest
          to the suggestible
          what the price of fish has to do
          with the marvel of hooey.

Pamela Alexander

NEST

Their little furs meet, make much
of each, you know the story, old
as hills, being silly up and down
the length of them. They get along

and then relapse. Autumn. Hard-headed
cyclists fly by in gangs; wasps
drift through the high white rooms
to bang against glass. Never learn.

Clouds smuggle the sun across, tea's
cold. They've lost their places in the books
on the bed, the bed's rucked up. Some
thing's humming that isn't them.

And rain. Worse, it's raining
wasps. Not the wings they want.

Pamela Alexander

SONG

Silence between moons. Notes
for the phoebe round in her nest.
Pitch of roof, pouch of twigs. Words

for nobody. Trees stir like this
for any creature, me or the doe I can't see.
She sees me. Trees wave in the dark.

Postcard with the message crossed out,
all picture. See the song? Earth plays
bass. The moon turns a corner.

Susan H. Case

PICTURE ROCKS WASH

My throat fatigues from the morning's silence
between us. In that time before the dissolution,
one hundred and three degrees.
We look for the hummingbird
nest. Wonder if it's true
they build new upon old—
the slur of years
a layer of debris
upon stolen spider webbing.
Last season, she built the nest too low
Sat unprotected.
            The straps
of my pack chafe.
I pause in the sand, tighten.
Your back gets small as you hurry
toward the break of rocks, a need,
even in this, to be the first. In my mind the well-
known contours of your face
already liquid, blurring.

Contributors

JOAN ALESHIRE grew up in Baltimore, Maryland. She has taught in the MFA Program at Waren Wilson College since 1983. Her fourth book of poems, *Litany of Thanks* was published in April 2003 by Four Way Books.

PAMELA ALEXANDER's work has appeared in *Mid-American Review*, *The Journal* and *Denver Quarterly*.

RONALD ALEXANDER's poems and stories have appeared in many journals. His novel, *The Final Audit*, was published by Hollyridge Press. He lives in Venice, California where he is at work on an historical novel set in a TB sanitorium in Indiana in the 1930's.

DICK ALLEN has published six collections of poetry, most recently *The Day Before: New Poems* from Sarabande Books in 2003 and *Ode to the Cold War: Poems New and Selected* (Sarabande, 1997). He has received poetry writing grants from the Ingram Merrill and NEA Foundations and has other new poems recently appearing in or forthcoming soon in *The Texas Review*, *The Hudson Review*, *The Atlantic Monthly*, *The Georgia Review*, among other periodicals.

JOE AMATO is the author of *Symptoms of a Finer Age* (Viet Nam Generation, 1994) and *Bookend: Anatomies of a Virtual Self* (SUNY Press, 1997). His latest collection of poetry, *Under Virga*, is forthcoming from Chax Press.

DOROTHY BARRESI's most recent book is *Rouge Pulp* (University of Pittsburgh, 2002).

JEANNE MARIE BEAUMONT is author of the poetry collections *Curious Conduct* (BOA, 2004) and *Placebo Effects* (Norton, 1997) as well as coeditor of *The Poets' Grimm: 20th Century Poems From Grimm Fairy Tales*. She teaches at Rutgers University and The Unterberg Poetry Center of the 92nd St. Y and lives in New York City.

CAL BEDIENT's books of poems are *Candy Necklace* (Wesleyan, 1997) and *The Violence of the Morning* (Georgia, 2002).

CARRIE BENNETT recently received her MFA in poetry from the Iowa Writers' Workshop. Her poetry is forthcoming in *So to Speak*, and currently appears in *The Bellingham Review*.

ANSELM BERRIGAN is the author of *Zero Star Hotel*, and has recently released a CD of poetry through Narrow House Recordings entitled "Pictures for Private Devotion."

MICHAEL C. BLUMENTHAL is the author of six books of poetry, most recently *Dusty Angel* (BOA Editions, 1999). His memoir, *All My Mothers And Fathers*, was published by Harper Collins in 2002. He lives in Paris and teaches at the Université François Rabelais in Tours.

CORNELL BRELLENTHIN's poetry recently appeared in *Slipstream* and she has won the *Cream City Review's* annual poetry contest. She is working on her creative dissertation (a novel set in Scandinavia during WWII) at the University of Wisconsin-Milwaukee.

GAYLORD BREWER is a professor at Middle Tennessee State University, where he founded and edits *Poems & Plays*. His most recent books of poems are *Four Nails* (Snail's Pace, 2001) and *Barbaric Mercies* (Red Hen, 2003)

JAMES BROCK has two books of poetry, *Nearly Florida* (Anhinga, 2000) and *The Sunshine Mine Accident* (University of Idaho, 1995). He teaches creative writing and literature at Florida Gulf Coast University, where he enjoys birding along the banks of the Caloosahatchee River.

RALPH BURNS' sixth book, *Ghost Notes*, won the *Field* Poetry Prize and was published in 2000 by Oberlin College Press. He teaches creative writing at the University of Arkansas at Little Rock.

SUSAN H. CASE is the author of the chapbook, *The Scottish Café* (Slapering Hol Press, 2002).

JAMES CERVANTES' poems have appeared recently in *The Laurel Review, The Boston Review, North American Review*, and other magazines. His books of poetry include *The Headlong Future* and *The Year Is Approaching Snow*, and *Live Music*, a chapbook of new poems from Pecan Grove Press. He is editor of the online journal *The Salt River Review*.

TOM CLARK is the author of many volumes of poetry, including *Empire of Skin* (Black Sparrow) and *White Thought* (Hard Press/The Figures), as well as a number of literary biographies, including *Jack Kerouac* (Thunder's Mouth), *Charles Olson: The Allegory of a Poet's Life* (North Atlantic) and *Edward Dorn: A World of Difference* (North Atlantic).

ADAM CLAY lives in Fayetteville, Arkansas. His poems have appeared in *Mississippi Review, Slipstream*, and *can we have our ball back?*

BRIAN CLEMENTS is the editor of *Sentence: A Journal of Prose Poetics* (info at http://firewheel-editions.org) and the author of *Essays Against Ruin*, a book of poems.

D.W. CUNNINGHAM was raised in Connecticut and now works as a writer in Maryland, near Washington, D.C. His poems have appeared in many small journals, recently *Seneca Review*, *Freshwater*, and *Shades of December* (online).

CATHERINE DALY is a poet and member of the National Book Critics Circle. Her book, *Locket*, is due from Tupelo Press in 2003. Another manuscript was a finalist in the National Poetry Series.

TENAYA DARLINGTON is the author of *Madame Deluxe* (Coffeehouse, 2000), winner of the National Poetry Series. She lives in Madison, Wisconsin where she is a columnist for Isthmus Newspaper and a crooner for the band Charlemagne.

JORDAN DAVIS lives down the hill from the Cloisters in New York City. He is the author of *Million Poems Journal* (Faux Press, 2003), and a reviewer for constantcritic.com.

JAMES DOYLE's most recent book *The Silk At Her Throat* (Cedar Hill Publications, 1999).

KARI EDWARDS is the author of *a day in the life of p.* (subpress collective 2002), *a diary of lies—Belladonna #27* by Balladonna Books (2002), and *obLiqUE paRt(itON): colLABorationS.* edwards' work can also be found in many journals including *Aufgabe*, *PuppyFlower*, *Vert*, *Narrativity*, *Shampoo*, *xStream*, *Big Bridge*, *AUGHT*, *Word/For Word*, *muse-apprentice-guild*, *5_Trope*, *Panic*, *Avoid Strange Men*, *Bird Dog Magazine*, *RealPoetik*, *Raised in a Barn* and *The International Journal of Sexuality and Gender Studies*.

ROGER FANNING's first book of poems, *The Island Itself*, was a National Poetry Series selection. His second book, *Homesick*, was published last year by Viking-Penguin. He currently teaches in the low-residency MFA Program for Writers at Warren Wilson, and lives in Seattle with his wife and son.

CHRIS FORHAN's book *The Actual Moon, The Actual Stars* won the Morse Prize and will be published by Northeastern University Press in the fall 2003. He teaches at Auburn.

RICHARD P. GABRIEL is a poet, essayist, and computer scientist. His most recent book is *Writers' Workshops and the Work of Making Things*.

GEOFFREY GATZA creates a kinetic neo-narrative american avant garde and is editor of the online journal *BlazeVOX2k3*. P. B. Gelly calls his chapbook, *Factory Manual*, "a sensitive display of illusion on the capital structures within contemporary American poetry." His artwork appears in *LOGOPOIEA*, *Beehive*, *Big Bridge*, *can we have our ball back*, *Blue Moon Review*, *Exquisite Corpse*, *xStream*, *VeRT*, and *Slope*.

MARK HALPERIN is the author of four volumes of poetry, the most recent of which is *Time As Distance* (New Issues, Western Michigan University, 2001). He lives with his wife and their dog near the trouty Yakima River.

DANIEL HALPERN is the author of eight collections of poems. He is editorial director of The Ecco Press, an imprint of HarperCollins. He has received many grants and awards, including fellowships from the Guggenheim Foundation and the National Endowment for the Arts.

MATT HART is a co-founder and editor of *Forklift Ohio: A Journal of Poetry, Cooking & Light Industrial Safety*. His work has appeared or is forthcoming in *Conduit, Ploughshares, Slope*, and other journals. He teaches at the Art Academy of Cincinnati.

MATTHEA HARVEY's first book is *Pity the Bathtub Its Forced Embrace of the Human Form*. Her second, *Sad Little Breathing Machine*, is forthcoming from Graywolf in 2004. She is the poetry editor of *American Letters & Commentary* and lives in Brooklyn.

WILLIAM HEYEN's poems have appeared in many journals including *The New Yorker, TriQuarterly, Poetry*, and *American Poetry Review*. Previous books include *Depth of Field, Long Island Light, Lord Dragonfly*, and *Erika: Poems of the Holocaust*.

AUGUST HIGHLAND is the originator of "Hyper-Literary Fiction" and the founder of the "Worldwide Literati Mobilization Network." He is also editor-in-chief of the *Muse-Apprentice-Guild*.

TONY HOAGLAND's third collection, *What Narcissism Means To Me* will be published in October 2003 by Graywolf Press. He teaches at the University of Houston.

ANN HUMPHREYS is a writer and singer living in Carrboro, North Carolina. For the past two years she has worked as an investigator, representing inmates of North Carolina's Death Row on appeal. Her EP, "Lucky Girl," will be coming out in early fall. She received her MFA from Warren Wilson College.

ROY JACOBSTEIN's book, *Ripe*, won the University of Wisconsin Press's 2002 Felix Pollak Prize after having been a finalist for the Academy of American Poets' Walt Whitman Award. His recent work has appeared or is forthcoming in *Triquarterly, The Threepenny Review, Prairie Schooner, Poetry Daily, Parnassus*, and *The Gettysburg Review* and received nominations for the 2002 and 2003 Pushcart Prizes. He is a public health physician working internationally in women's reproductive health.

HALVARD JOHNSON has published four collections of poetry: *The Dance of the Red Swan, Transparencies and Projections, Eclipse*, and *Winter Journey*, all from New Rivers Press and, now out of print, archived at the Contemporary American Poetry Archives <http://capa.conncoll.edu>. His poetry and fiction have appeared in *Puerto del Sol, Wisconsin Review, Mudfish, Poetry: New York, For Poetry, CrossConnect, Salt River*

Review, Blue Moon Review, Crania, Gulf Stream, The Florida Review and *Synaesthetic.* Currently, he resides in New York City with his wife, the prize-winning fiction writer and painter Lynda Schor. He teaches from time to time at the Eugene Lang College of the New School University and in Newark, New Jersey, at the New Jersey Institute of Technology.

PATRICIA SPEARS JONES is an award-winning poet and author of the collection, *The Weather That Kills* (Coffee House Press, 1995) and the play "Mother" produced by Mabou Mines. Her work has been widely published with appearances in *Best American Poetry 2000, Bomb, Agni, Barrow Street, Ploughshares* and *The Village Voice.*

RICHARD JONES is the author of *The Blessing: New And Selected Poems* (Copper Canyon Press), which won the Society of Midland Authors Award for Poetry for 2000.

LEWIS LaCOOK is the author of *Drowning In The Age Of Mid-Air,* an e-book from xPress(ed), (2002; http://www.xpressed.org/). His work has appeared in many journals including *3rd Bed, Big Bridge,* and *5_Trope.*

PETER LEVITT is a poet and translator who received a Lannan Foundation Literary Award in Poetry. His book, *Writing Spirit,* was published by Harmony Books (2003).

GERALD LOCKLIN's next full-length book will be *The Pocket Book: Novella and Stories,* from Water Row Press in late 2003. His most recent full-length collection is *The Life Force Poems* (Water Row Press, 2002). He has taught English at California State University, Long Beach, since 1965.

THOMAS LUX's most recent book is *The Street of Clocks* (Mariner Books, 2003). He is the Bourne Professor of Poetry at the Georgia Institute of Technology.

K. SILEM MOHAMMAD lives and teaches in Santa Cruz, California. His new book of poetry is titled *Deer Head Nation* (Tougher Disguises, 2003). He also runs a poetry blog, *lime tree,* at http://limetree.blogspot.com.

ELISABETH MURAWSKI is the author of *Moon and Mercury* (Washington Writers' Publishing House, 1990) and *Troubled by an Angel* (Cleveland State University Poetry Center, 1997). Her poems have appeared in numerous journals and magazines, including *Hayden's Ferry Review, The New Republic, Grand Street, American Poetry Review, Virginia Quarterly Review, Shenandoah,* and *Quarterly West.*

JASON NELSON is almost exclusively creating hypermedia works as push button phones do not seem nearly as threatening. This might be his last print publication. For a bit of digiwork: http://www.heliozoa.com/search.html.

HARRY NUDEL was born in 1946 in a displaced person's camp 15 miles from Auschwitz. He came to the United States in 1949 where he attended Bronx High School of Science, CCNY, studying with Paul Blackburn, and then earned his Ph.D.

at SUNY Buffalo, working with Robert Creeley. He works as a bookseller. Over the last 5 years, his writing has appeared almost exclusively on the internet.

LOUIS PHILLIPS is a poet, playwright, and short-story writer. SMU Press published his collection of stories, *A Dream Where No One Dare Lives*, and Fort Schuyler Press will soon publish his new collection of stories, *The Bus to the Moon*. He has published over 35 books for children and adults.

CHUCK ROSENTHAL's most recent novel is *My Mistress, Humanity* (Hollyridge Press, 2002).

LEE ROSSI is the author of *Beyond Rescue*. His work has appeared in the anthologies *Grand Passion, Truth & Lies That Press for Life*, and *New Los Angeles Poets*, as well as in journals such as *The Sun, Poetry East, Chelsea, The Wormwood Review, Poetry/LA* and *The Los Angeles Times*. He has also served as editor of the early 90's poetry magazine *Tsunami* and on the Organizing Committee of the Los Angeles Poetry Festival.

ALAN SONDHEIM's books include the anthology *Being on Line: Net Subjectivity* (Lusitania, 1996), *Disorders of the Real* (Station Hill, 1988), and *.echo* (alt-X digital arts, 2001). His video and films have been shown internationally. Sondheim co-moderates several email lists, including Cybermind, Cyberculture, and Wryting and is currently Associate Editor of the online magazine Beehive. Sondheim teaches in the trAce online writing program, and this year is at Florida International University in Miami. Sondheim lives in Brooklyn; he lectures and publishes widely on contemporary art and Internet issues.

GARY SULLIVAN is the author of *How to Proceed in the Arts* (Faux Press, 2001) and, with Nada Gordon, *Swoon* (Granary Books, 2001). He and Gordon co-edit the Poetry Project Newsletter. His serialized cartoon, "The New Life," appears regularly in *Rain Taxi*.

ALICE TEMPLETON's poems have appeared in *Poetry, Puerto del Sol, Kalliope*, and elsewhere. She is also the author of a critical study of Adrienne Rich's poetics, entitled *The Dream and the Dialogue* (University of Tennessee Press, 1994).

CAMMY THOMAS' poems have appeared in *Marlboro Review, Pine Island Journal, Mystic River Review*, and elsewhere. Her first book, *Inheritance*, will be published in 2005 by Four Way Books. She has a PhD in English from Berkeley and an MFA from Warren Wilson College, and teaches English at Concord Academy in Concord, Massachusetts.

DAVID WAGONER has published seventeen books of poems, most recently *The House Of Song* (University of Illinois Press, 2002), and ten novels, one of which, *The Escape Artist*, was made into a movie by Francis Ford Coppola. He has taught at the University of Washington since 1954 and was the editor of *Poetry Northwest* until its end in 2002.

ROSMARIE WALDROP's most recent book of poems is *Reluctant Gravities* (New Directions, 1999). *Blindsight* (New Directions) and *Love, like Pronouns* (Omnidawn) are forthcoming in 2003. Her memoir, *Lavish Absence: Recalling and Rereading Edmond Jabès*, is just out from Wesleyan University Press. She lives in Providence, Rhode Island where she co-edits Burning Deck books with Keith Waldrop.

JESSE WATERS teaches English at the University of North Carolina at Wilmington. A 2002 Pushcart nominee and 2001 *River Styx International* selection by Billy Collins, his work has appeared or is forthcoming in such journals as *The Adirondack Review*, *Cimarron Review, Sycamore Review* and *Magma*.

ELEANOR WILNER's most recent book is *Reversing The Spell; New & Selected Poems* (Copper Canyon, 1998). She teaches in the MFA Program for Writers at Warren Wilson College.

GAIL WRONSKY is the author of two books of poetry, *Dying for Beauty* (Copper Canyon, 2000) and *Again the Gemini Are in the Orchard* (BrickHouse Books, 1991). Her poems and critical essays have appeared in *Antioch Review, Denver Quarterly, Colorado Review, Boston Review, Virginia Quarterly Review* and other journals. She is the recipient of an Artists Fellowship from the California Arts Council. Her first novel, *The Love-talkers*, was published by Hollyridge Press.

GERALD YELLE, a New England native, lives in Amherst. A University of Massachusetts MFA, he teaches high school English. Recent poems have appeared in *The Temple* and *The Lucid Stone*.

"A beautifully written, brilliant, deeply philosophical novel."
— **Chuck Kinder**

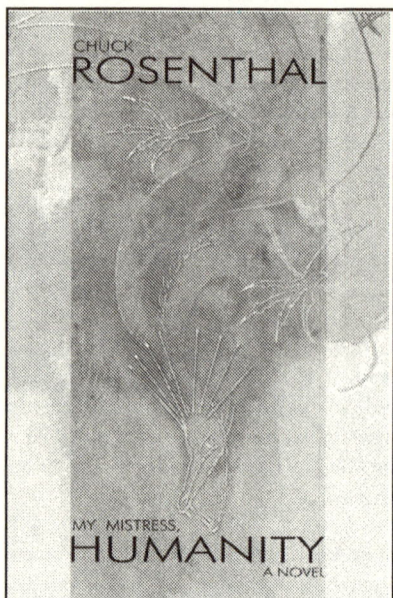

MY MISTRESS, HUMANITY
A Novel
by CHUCK ROSENTHAL

ISBN 0-9676003-5-9
$17.95 Softcover

Not far in the future a series of catastrophic weather events have crippled the technological infrastructure of the world and humankind is on the verge of total annihilation. One man knows the secret and only one young woman can save the planet. From Chuck Rosenthal comes an apocalyptic vision of the future, *My Mistress, Humanity*. Rosenthal's gothic vision of the future is both terrifying and beautiful. In the gorgeous lyric prose for which he's known, like the creator of a modern-day Frankenstein, Rosenthal takes us on a journey towards humanity's ultimate destruction and redemption.

Hollyridge Press

"You will be dazzled and amazed."
— **David St. John**

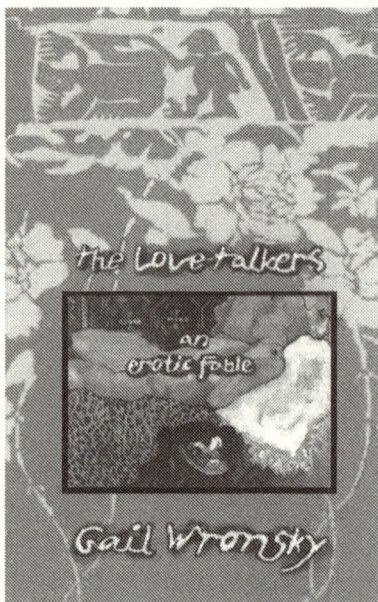

THE LOVE-TALKERS
An Erotic Fable
by GAIL WRONSKY

ISBN 0-9676003-3-2
$23.95 Hardcover

The beauty of Gail Wronsky's poetic language has never been better displayed than in *The Love-talkers*. Mexico City, with its parks and cathedrals provides a lush backdrop for the story. A sumptuously rendered book, celebrating passionate imagination with all the sublime joy of physical love, Wronsky's elegiac style summons up the magic of Latin American fiction in this novel of desire which brings us into the depths of erotic charge. From ecstatic awakenings to feverish enactments of appetite, Wronsky's novel reveals what happens when we find our deepest yearnings made true.

Hollyridge Press

"An amazing use of language and clarity
of description compels the reader on."
—**Patricia Gulian**, *Book/Mark*

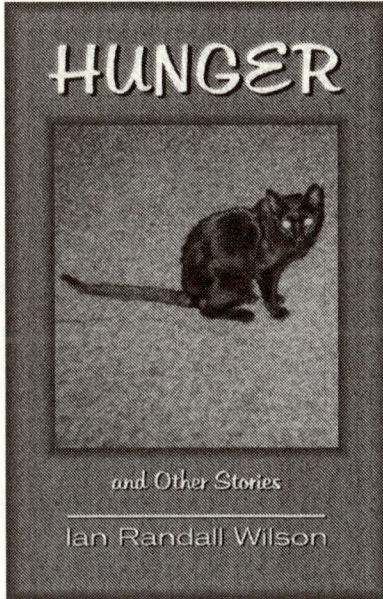

HUNGER
and Other Stories
by Ian Randall Wilson

ISBN 0-9676003-0-8
$12.95 Paperback

In his first collection of short stories, Ian Randall Wilson's characters are driven by intense yearnings for the satisfaction of their most basic human desires. All are thwarted by personal shortcomings, or the shortcomings of others, in their attempts to fulfill their longing. Here are 14 stories which "despite their restlessness," former *North American Review* editor Robley Wilson says, "glitter with persistent hopes."

Hollyridge Press

"Alexander is an accomplished writer with
a deft hand for characterization."
— **Hillary Johnson**, *LA Weekly*

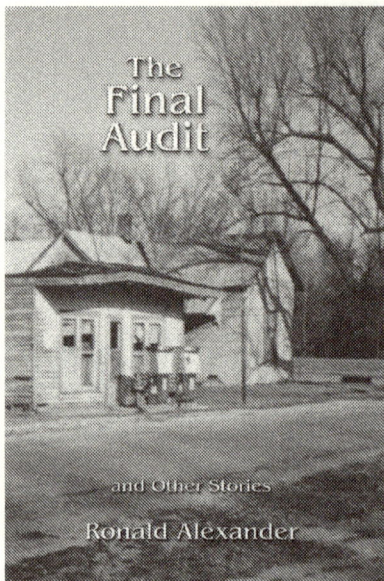

THE FINAL AUDIT
and Other Stories
by Ronald Alexander

ISBN 0-9676003-1-6
$12.95 Paperback

In Ronald Alexander's debut novel, Dexter Giles lives a double life, balancing a straight-jacketed career in the homophobic towers of corporate culture with his secret world as a gay man. Nancy Lamb writes, "The interconnected stories in this novel are serious and unforgettable and told with humor and insight. Alexander displays an intuitive grasp of the complexity of family relationships and the power of long-term friendships."

Hollyridge Press

"Among the new magazines. . .one of the best has to be *88*."
—*Literary Magazine Review*

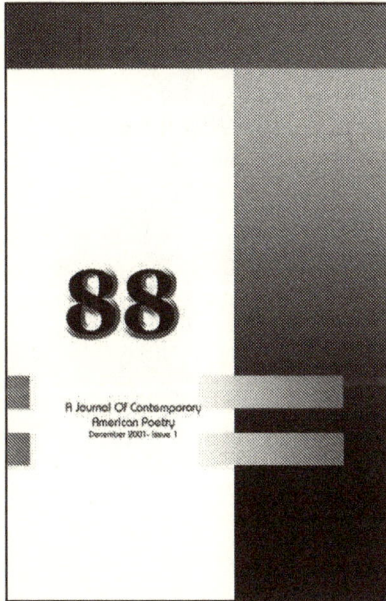

88
A Journal of Contemporary
American Poetry (Issue 1)
Denise L. Stevens (editor)

ISBN 0-9676003-4-0
$13.95 Paperback

Issue 1 features an amazing range of poetry:
—The wonderfully comic sensibilities of Amiri Baraka: "I get horrible letters / From Ghosts / Demanding / Money."
—Dean Young writes in an echo of the New York School: "I don't ask for much: a little cleavage, / the honey of deconstruction to go along / with my cereal but something's scorched / my curtsey, one of my eyes's funny."
—Roger Weingarten's poignant narrative poem about fathers: "Into the no man's land / behind the flimsy curtain of my / resolve not to let them / get to me."
—Postmodernism from Gail Wronsky: "She's // greasy as a melancholy rhyme. What / self-esteems are   each day, paradoxically, / dismantled in her beehive?"
Plus essays and reviews. . .

Hollyridge Press

www.hollyridgepress.com

THE BEST IN AMERICAN POETRY!

88

A Journal of Contemporary
American Poetry (Issue 2)
Ian Randall Wilson (editor)

ISBN 0-9676003-6-7
$13.95 Paperback

Including the work of:

Barry Ballard	Jim Barnes	Bill Berkson
Killarney Clary	Patricia Corbus	Stephen Corey
Stuart Dischell	Richard Garcia	Reginald Gibbons
Joy Gladding	Elton Glaser	Rachel Hadas
Jonathan Holden	Mark Jarman	Kate Knapp Johnson
Peter Johnson	Carolyn Lei-lanilau	Gerald Locklin
Fred Moramarco	Elisabeth Murawski	Mary Ruefle
Ron Silliman	Alan Sondheim	Terese Svoboda
James Tate	Elaine Terranova	Susan Wheeler
Charles Harper Webb	Eve Wood	Gail Wronsky

Plus reviews. . .

Hollyridge Press

Guidelines

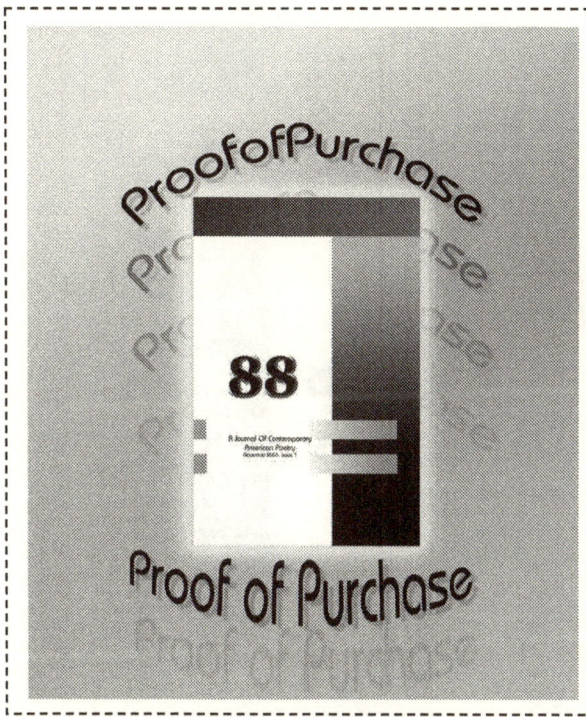

Submission Guidelines

Unsolicited submissions will be considered March 1 through May 31 only. Unsolicited submissions postmarked outside that window will be returned unread. However, submissions accompanied by an original proof-of-purchase will be considered year round.

Manuscripts must be limited to five poems per submission with author name and address appearing on each page. Long poems not exceeding ten single spaced typewritten pages will be considered, but poems longer than three pages must be submitted separately.

Essays and reviews will also be considered. Please limit essays to no more than ten pages, double-spaced. Reviews must be no more than eight double-spaced pages.

At this time, material is being considered via USPS submission only. No disk, email or fax submissions. (However, if accepted, material must be provided later on disk.)

Include a self-addressed, stamped envelope for return of manuscripts. Submissions without SASE will be discarded unread. Cover letter with short bio, please. No simultaneous submissions or previously published material will be considered. We report on submissions within one to three months.

Mail submissions to: Editor, 88, c/o Hollyridge Press, P. O. Box 2872, Venice, CA 90294

Guidelines

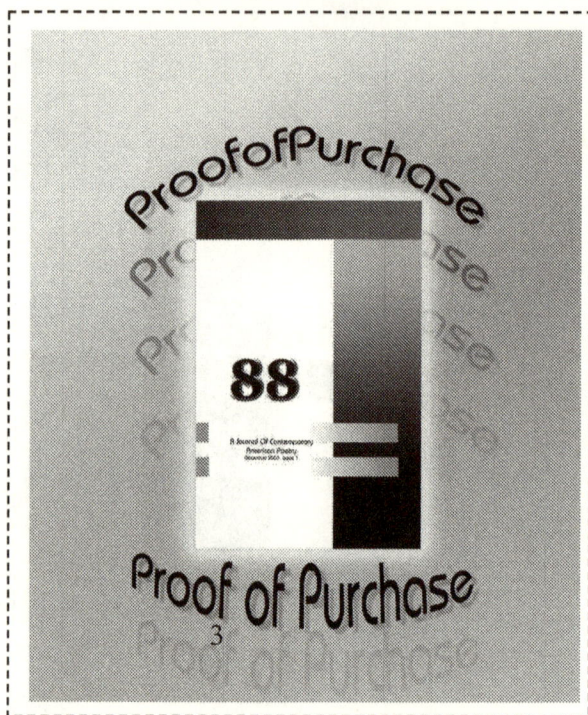

Submission Guidelines

Unsolicited submissions will be considered March 1 through May 31 only. Unsolicited submissions postmarked outside that window will be returned unread. However, submissions accompanied by an original proof-of-purchase will be considered year round.

Manuscripts must be limited to five poems per submission with author name and address appearing on each page. Long poems not exceeding ten single spaced typewritten pages will be considered, but poems longer than three pages must be submitted separately.

Essays and reviews will also be considered. Please limit essays to no more than ten pages, double-spaced. Reviews must be no more than eight double-spaced pages.

At this time, material is being considered via USPS submission only. No disk, email or fax submissions. (However, if accepted, material must be provided later on disk.)

Include a self-addressed, stamped envelope for return of manuscripts. Submissions without SASE will be discarded unread. Cover letter with short bio, please. No simultaneous submissions or previously published material will be considered. We report on submissions within one to three months.

Mail submissions to: Editor, 88, c/o Hollyridge Press, P. O. Box 2872, Venice, CA 90294

www.ingramcontent.com/pod-product-compliance
Lightning Source LLC
LaVergne TN
LVHW011351080426
835511LV00005B/240